IDEOLOGY AND
COMMUNITY ACTION

IDEOLOGY AND COMMUNITY ACTION

The West Side Organization of Chicago, 1964-67

by

Bernard O. Brown

Center for the Scientific Study of Religion

Chicago, Illinois

STUDIES IN RELIGION AND SOCIETY

Center for the Scientific Study of Religion

For a complete list of the publications in the series, see the back of the book.

Center for the Scientific Study of Religion
5757 University Avenue
Chicago, Illinois 60637

I S B N: Cloth: 0-913348-16-3
            Paper: 0-913348-17-1

Library of Congress Catalog Card Number: 77-91842

IDEOLOGY AND COMMUNITY ACTION

The West Side Organization of Chicago,
1964-67

by

Bernard O. Brown

Center for the Scientific Study of Religion

Chicago, Illinois

STUDIES IN RELIGION AND SOCIETY

Center for the Scientific Study of Religion

For a complete list of the publications in the
series, see the back of the book.

Center for the Scientific Study of Religion
5757 University Avenue
Chicago, Illinois 60637

I S B N: Cloth: 0-913348-16-3
            Paper: 0-913348-17-1

Library of Congress Catalog Card Number: 77-91842

of the 1960s. The changes which have occurred in that community
and in the larger society have shifted public attention away from
the problems, and their proposed solutions, which WSO identified
and represented. Yet the economic realities for those people who
were the original constituency of that small community organization
have not changed. Welfare rolls have increased. Unemployment among
young black men remains very high. And the obscurity of persons
who have no organized means of access to the public sphere is
pervasive.

The first chapter of this study attempts to place the story
within an ongoing discussion of the cultural determinants of social
organization among the very poor. Chapters two through six contain
narrations of WSO activity during the middle years of the decade.
The final chapter is an analysis of the interpretive process in
which WSO was engaged in its public activities, a process which the
study itself attempts to advance and to exemplify.

Bernard O. Brown

PREFACE

On September 2, 1975, three Chicago daily newspapers reported the arrest of four men on a charge of selling illegal narcotics to an undercover agent of the Metropolitan Enforcement Group. All of them were employees, including the Director, of the West Side Organization Drug Abuse and Rehabilitation Center. The next day arrest warrants were served on two other men associated with the program. The Regional Office of the Department of Health, Education and Welfare announced at once a full investigation of the administration of government funds by the West Side Organization in its rehabilitation programs. The amount of money received by this community group was reported to have been in excess of 1.6 million dollars. The organization had also been awarded grants by various private foundations.

The six persons named in the charge of illegal sale were not active in the West Side Organization during the years of this study, 1964-67. However, the leadership of the group was largely the same in 1975 as in 1965. Therefore, the legal difficulties which have resulted from the arrests, the unfavorable publicity attendant upon the incident, and the investigation of how funds were spent all touch some of those persons who figure importantly in the story I tell in the following pages. My purpose is not to throw light on what has happened in the intervening years, but to provide an interpretation of what WSO was and did within the context of a particular period of our recent history. The fact that WSO became, in later years, an agency of "Black Capitalism" in the community, operating oil stations, fast food franchises and other businesses, and that it became adept at tapping governmental and foundation sources for its various programs, is not anticipated in the account which follows.

In the 1960s WSO was responsive to a public mood which focused attention upon WSO's modest attempts to express the sensibilities of the ghetto poor and to generate actions on their behalf. In the years following 1968, the interests of civic leaders, the news business, and the general public turned elsewhere. The activities of civil rights leaders and community organizations were also directed to other ends. The original goals of WSO as a community organization of the unemployed and welfare poor were redefined and its efforts were redirected, away from campaigning against institutions that symbolized the economic futility of their situation, and toward grasping opportunities for a few of their number to improve their economic position. If WSO was opportunistic in sensing the openings provided by the vagrant spirit of social reform in the 1960s, it was not less attuned to the temper of the times in the 1970s. In ways consonant with their much larger base and constituency, Chicago organizations like Operation PUSH and The Woodlawn Organization accomplished a similar turn in the years following the decline of the civil rights movement.

I believe that it is now important to understand what an organization such as WSO attempted to do in the turbulent context

TABLE OF CONTENTS

IDEOLOGY AND COMMUNITY ACTION

CHAPTER I

INTRODUCTION

It has been argued by the sociologist, Michael Clarke, among others, that the ideology of persons in modern Western nations who share a liberal, reformist, consensualist image of their society, will admit no intermediate proposals for the amelioration of social problems which fall between the polar extremes of reform and revolution.[1] The reason is that repressive measures of *any* degree are seen to operate destructively upon the consensual basis of their society. Liberal minded persons are said to be incapable of understanding those who operate against the liberal consensus and outside the accepted processes of reform, except as revolutionaries. Persons and groups who express social discontent may not have guns, or even want guns. They may follow the law scrupulously, or recognize its sovereignty by careful and deliberate acts of civil disobedience. But they occupy no intermediate position within the ideology of the liberal elites, because there is none. They are labeled as revolutionaries, with the help of the ubiquitous public media.

Clarke argues that there are no intermediate ideological positions for social protesters because the political and economic *interests* of the elites allow for none. Yet one could argue that even economic self-interest might well lead to the discernment of the relative economic advantage of mildly repressive action as opposed to revolutionary destruction. The real point of Clarke's data on liberal elites is that their ideology operates as a culturally formal cause to restrict options.

Clarke's example reveals the undoubted fact that the action of labeling a group as deviant from an ideological norm partakes of a political struggle. His paper concerns the types of labels which a ruling elite apply to the non-elites who constitute the "problem" within the existing social order. He finds that these labels associate as types. When a group is operating against the liberal social order from motives that can be regarded as deliberate, the appropriate labels assigned to them will associate in a cluster of terms that connote *revolution*. When a group acts without deliberate motive, but from some external compulsion, the symbols applied to them associate as *mob*. When an individual actor is considered in these deviant terms, the labels associate as *criminal* when the act is deliberate, and *sick* when it is determined. Thus Clarke presents a four-fold classification of types:

	COLLECTIVE	INDIVIDUAL
DELIBERATE	Revolutionary	Criminal
DETERMINED	Mob	Sick

3

The typology is elaborated, though not altered fundamentally from an ideological standpoint, when distinctions are introduced reflecting a more sophisticated understanding first of social groups; between the revolutionary collectivities and criminal individuals one can identify intentional groups of a more organized character, i.e., gangs. Second, a liberal moral consciousness enables distinctions to be made from perspectives which are"scientifically"informed when anti-social behavior is not willed, but determined, as opposed to a moralistic perspective. The ideology of deviance allows for slum residents to be grouped moralistically as members of mobs, or "scientifically," as victims of social pathology who manifest forms of group sickness. The individuals thus identified are seen as depraved persons, or as sick. Clarke's more elaborate table then reads as follows:

	COLLECTIVITY	ORGANIZATION	INDIVIDUAL	
				Maximum threat ↑
DELIBERATE	Revolution	Gang	Criminal	Evil
DETERMINED				
Moral	Slum	Mob	Depraved	
Scientific	Social pathology	Group sickness, e.g., mass hysteria, group neurosis	Sick	Pathetic ↓
Maximum threat ←				→ Minimum threat

Contagion Potential

The deviance syndrome is sustained throughout, though with these "scientific" distinctions the behavior is better "understood."
Clarke has focused on the ideological position of "ruling elites" in a liberal modern Western society who see restive non-elites as "the problem." In my work, I have tried to describe and interpret the ideology of some of the people who were seen as "the problem."
The differences go beyond the simple choice of focus. The task of providing public symbols by which a group of people recognize and express their own interests and beliefs requires an instrument which assimilates, focuses, formulates and reflects those meanings in ideological forms. For the dominant elites of our culture the public media are highly superior and efficient instruments. Many other institutions of our complex society perform this service also. The non-elites, however, must either accept the version of themselves that is formulated so powerfully through all of these culturally acceptable means, or they must devise other ways of assimilating, focusing, formulating, and reflecting their own understandings. My study concentrates upon a small ghetto community organization which, in the 1960s, was engaged in this process of formulating and expressing a counter-ideology, and which

became thereby a defining instrument of the social world of non-
elites.
    Because Clarke was dealing with a powerful elite which had
superior access to the means by which its ideology was formulated
and promulgated, one would expect, and one finds, a much sharper
ideological focus emerging in his work--that is, the ideological
labels associate more readily, and the categories formed seem much
more clearly related to political and economic interest factors.
My study concerns an ideology which, though certainly drawn from
sub-cultural strata of meaning in the associative life of the
ghetto communities, was (at the time of the study) at a nascent
stage of emergence into the view of the wider society. The study
concentrates upon an ideology being shaped and promulgated for
wider public consumption. The organization leaders were aware that
the public media and the other institutional means of action in
"The Great Society"--business organizations, churches, unions,
government bureaucracies, police, courts, and others--were suddenly
quite interested in what their people felt and thought about a
great many issues. Their claim to leadership and attention was
their representativeness. They needed confirmation from the people
among whom they lived that they spoke in the accents of the community. They sought for and found access to certain centers of
power. It was this dual process of identifying and articulating
the ideology of a marginal community which drew my attention in
1966 to the West Side Organization for Full Employment in Chicago.
    WSO, located on the Near West Side of Chicago's loop was, in
1964, an early and important experiment in community organization
because it was a test case of an attempt to organize and to empower
the poorest residents of a community, using their own resources of
leadership, with very slight input of leadership and funds from
beyond the neighborhood itself. WSO sought to involve individuals
in leadership roles, unemployed young men and welfare mothers,
whose social condition could have been described and analyzed from
a number of perspectives, none of which would have been considered
promising for the emergence of leadership, or for the formation of
programs and structures of accountability which would lead into
several sectors of society. The available images of who these
persons were and what their prospects might be associated quite
readily in the categories of ideology that Clarke constructed.
They were regarded as unemployable rejects of the productive society, the criminal element of a slum neighborhood, street bums and
addicts, hopelessly dependent and morally irresponsible public
charges. These images, usually accepted and seemingly accurate,
provided no means whatsoever by which positive self-identity could
flourish or group initiative occur. But alternative images of
these individuals and their common situation, though they certainly
existed in the associative life of the people in the neighborhoods,
were not formulated as representations of persons acting together
and addressing the surrounding society from a position of some
strength. This is what the community organization attempted to do.
    The 1960s and early 1970s were years in which a great deal of
attention was paid in the sociological literature to the questions
of a "culture of poverty." The debate concerned the alleged existence of value structures, patterned "recipes for living," which
are intrinsic to the communities of the chronic poor.[2] If these
cultures of poverty existed, then it could be reliably argued that

the cultural preferences of the poor were themselves major impair-
ments in their capacity to rise from poverty. One strain of this
literature was concerned, naturally enough, with the attitudes of
the chronically poor toward work.

This aspect of the "culture of poverty" debate is summarized
nicely in Norman Bonney's paper, "Work and Ghetto Culture."[3] The
issue he identified could be formulated as follows: if it is true
that chronically poor persons often demonstrate in the jobs they
hold a poor adjustment to the requirements of steady and remuner-
ative employment--i.e., by their frequent absence from work,
tardiness, insufficient commitment to the task, etc.--is this because work itself interferes with value preferences characteristic
of street life in the ghetto--i.e., the lure of excitement, weak
ties with families, the immediacy of contact with friends, the
desire to seek rather than to defer gratifications? Or is it more
accurate to characterize the fundamental values of the poor as
identical with the rest of society--the desire for stability, recognition of achievement, growing financial rewards and responsibil-
ities--and to account for the behavior that is dysfunctional for
these goals as the responses of persons who have learned to accept
constant frustration and denial as their expected lot in life? Or
is there a position intermediary between these two theories? Bonney
finds that there is, and that his own research among the chronically
unemployed in Chicago sustains the middle position. He writes:

> The most acceptable formulations of the relationship between culture
> and situational incentives in the black lower class . . . recognize
> the existence of a distinctive ghetto sub-culture and emphasize that
> it is not a totally isolated system but rather exists in co-existence
> and tension alongside a conventional culture whose influence extends
> into the ghetto. Individual actors are exposed to both systems, can
> become committed more or less to one at any one time or switch between
> them as their careers develop. . . . In the work sphere the individual
> actor is confronted with two competing orientations to the world of
> work--the conventional norms of mainstream society and the deviant
> values of the street sub-culture.[4]

I find that my reading in this material and my own research
leads me to a conclusion which differs importantly with any of the
positions summarized above, although it can be understood best in
relation to Bonney's argument. As my work concentrates upon the
process of ideological formulation, I am clearly within that range
of discussion on the effect of relative cultural values upon work
patterns. But it is important to ask what effect there may be upon
such a distinctive ghetto sub-cultural orientation as Bonney finds
when a group of ghetto men attempt to penetrate the world of conventional work and business culture, not as individuals trying to
make it on their own in the world of work, not as entrepreneurs
themselves (the so-called Black Capitalism phase of WSO activity
came after the period of this study), but as advocates and ideological spokesmen for those whose sub-culture exists in tension with
conventional culture. My conclusion will not support the view of
Banfield and others that there is a distinctive and relatively
impermeable ethos of the poor which constitutes a critical impair-
ment to change. Instead, I will argue that communal structures

which offer access to the dominant culture offer as well the means
to reassess and reformulate a relativistic cultural position.

Ideological expressions are a kind of moral language in which
social judgments are made with reference to persons "outside" as
well as "inside" the social group. When these expressions are
ignored or suppressed, they rigidify. It then becomes necessary
to defend the interests identified within the ideology, which
means to defend the terms of identification themselves. But the
creation of a language of moral judgments is inherently a public
action. Its meanings are not self-elucidating, but depend upon a
context of meaning that extends beyond the boundaries of the group
in which they were coined. To quote the theologian, H. Richard
Niebuhr,

> The societies that judge, or in which we judge ourselves, are self-
> transcending societies. And the process of self-transcendence . . .
> does not come to rest until the total community of being has been
> involved.[5]

This study concerns the attempts of a group of actors to establish
the terms of a moral relationship with those inside *and* outside
of their community.

It is my own position that the process of formulating these
relationships by a community of persons who have lived in circumstances straitened by extreme poverty and racial discrimination,
and obscured by images of their being which deny their human
capacities of self-transcendence, is a process essential to liber-
ation. But the process would not be truly liberating if the result were a new closed system of meanings. The process of cultural formulation must be portrayed in its inherently self-
transcending nature, which means that these movements toward the
creation of new symbols of communal identity, new ideologies expressive of what is and what ought to be within the social world,
must be evaluated in terms of an ethic of interpretation.

There is, after all, no such thing as an unmediated, uninter-
preted fact about the social world. The community organization
movement was committed to fostering and enhancing, by various
methods, the interpretations that emerge from the unified actions
of heretofore powerless and obscure persons. The organizational
task was to enable these persons and groups to interact with the
sources of meaning internal to their own lives and constitutive of
their lives in the wider context of the social world. The goal
has been to enhance their human capacities to create a cohesive
social and communal entity in contact with other communities.

The Method of the Study

Briefly stated, I have organized the data I gathered during
several months of participant observation in WSO into forms which
accentuate the function of symbolic display in the behavior of
leaders. I have relied, to some extent, upon a theory of "dramatistic analysis," which is the creation of the distinguished
literary and social critic, Kenneth Burke, and which has been
advocated as a method of analyzing symbolic forms of social relations by Hugh Dalziel Duncan and William H. Rueckert.[6] A quotation

from Duncan's *Symbols in Society* states succinctly the justification
for an interest in symbolic display.

> Social groups must stage themselves before audiences whose approval
> legitimizes their power. Audiences, in turn, must see the problems
> of the community acted out in some kind of dramatic presentation, for
> it is only through the forms created in such action that community
> problems become comprehensible as *actions*. We learn to act, not
> simply by preparing to act, or by thinking "about" action, but by
> playing roles in various kinds of dramas. . . . The staging of roles
> in dramatic structures is . . . a staging, or presentation, of our-
> selves to public and private audiences whose approval gives us a
> sense of identity or belonging.[7]

The data are cast into dramatic forms which are intended to
reveal the symbolic character of certain of WSO's actions in the
public sphere. This is not to say their only significance is as
rites enacted for the sake of establishing and authenticating a
position of leadership. But WSO was clearly chartered as a group
intended to enact public representations of meanings which were
indigenous to a victimized sector of the urban population. WSO's
chosen constituency was not only essentially powerless to affect
its own public interests, but had existed as socially invisible,
except to those public and private agencies of the society devoted
to providing custodial and ameliorative attention to the victims.
WSO was designed to create and enact leadership roles. The
setting for that enactment was familiar to citizens who were rea-
sonably well-informed about what we now call institutional racism
in the cities. But the dimensions of the representative role to
be assumed were unknown even to the most experienced advisors of
WSO in its period of foundation.
To portray a role is to enact to the best of one's understanding
the meanings, expectations, and implications attached to the role.
In most social situations the requirements of the role are routinely
acknowledged. Provided that they are within the competence of the
actor, they are readily and unreflectively assumed. One is hardly
aware of having donned a particular set of characterizations, man-
ners, or traditions associated with a social role.
But in a situation where a role is, in a real sense, being
created even as it is being assumed, one can expect to observe a
kind of acting with a high degree of self-consciousness of the
meaning it bears. We can expect to see people being very sensitive to what adheres to the role of "representative leader" in the
new situation.
The importance of role theory within dramatistic analysis is
based on the belief that for most people the order of relationships
within society is personified and not abstractly maintained. That
is, the roles which are enacted are meant to exemplify principles
of order, which are themselves being sustained by public enactment
or introduced as alternatives to an old order.
Social symbols express ordered relationships which must be
publicly rehearsed at whatever moments it is deemed necessary that
they be upheld, destroyed, or altered for the good of the social
order itself.

From a sociological view, the drama of community is a drama of authority, a struggle by those in power, or those seeking power, to control
symbols already powerful, or to create new symbols that will make
orderly those relationships which cannot be made orderly through the
use of traditional or sacred symbols.[8]

The emphasis upon roles ought not to preclude examination of
other symbolizations that occur in social drama. Important also
are motivational elements perceived as implicit within what is
"given" in the social environment. The nature of the stage, or the
situation, is expressed, of course, in symbols, and it becomes
possible to advance explanations of the social order which are de-
rived more or less exclusively from various conceptions of the
"given situation." Duncan suggests that purely environmental explanations of the social order are like explanations "of the playing
of the game by the shape of the playing field."[9] There is no question of the influence upon the game of baseball of the shape of
the infield diamond, for example. But the "givenness" of that
shape is affected by interpretations of its possible uses, limitations, etc. It is not the same reality for a team dependent upon
its defensive abilities as it is for a team with outstanding
pitchers that can afford to play its best hitters in the regular
lineup, whether or not they are the best infielders available. The
differentiation in "the given" is precisely the size of the hole
that appears between second base and short stop. So dramatistic
analysis is interested in the organization given to the stage, or
situation, by publicly shared interpretations of what is given.

The most crucial concern of dramatistic analysis is to discover symbolizations of the fitness of the means to the act.
Actions which represent public meanings will press toward fulfill-
ing the sense of "rightness" in what is done. The motivation of
action is to persuade and to achieve social cohesion within the
meaning of the act. We are touching here upon the public function
of art. Dramatistic analysis recognizes the suasive power resident
in the public sense of what is fitting in the way something is done.

Finally, we may be able to discover those symbolic intimations
of a final cause, a perfection of what is present to human experience in its imperfect forms. Human action will express notions of
perfection, if only through symbols which press for some transcen-
dence of previous meanings and justifications. Duncan and Burke
call this symbolic function "mounting"--the means by which the
symbolically real is continuously and successively transcended until
comprehended by a final principle of the ultimate perfection and
power.

In summary, an analysis of social action in the mode of
symbolic display would consider meanings as expressed in symbols
of 1) the given situation, 2) the means, 3) the roles (inherited
and transformed), 4) the forms of action, and 5) the principle of
perfection.

In addition, the dramaturgical model requires sensitivity in
analysis to those conceptualizations of audience which are symbolically represented within the action. For whom is the action dis-
played? What audience is addressed with the intention of persuasion? The possibilities which Duncan discerns are:

1) the general public, or publics

2)   the community guardians

3)   individuals treated as confidants and advisors

4)   the inward self

5)   the Ideal or Ultimate Person of address

Dramatistic analysis thus casts the data of social interaction into the forms of art drama. The purpose is heuristic--to open to inquiry the ends, purposes, and values which are present in symbolizations of social reality. The art drama form is appropriate because the realm of art is dynamic. One expects to observe the symbols of what is real, valuable, and eternally valid being subjected to change, ambiguity, doubt, and argument. Duncan writes:

> In art we institutionalize doubt, not only through logical analysis,
> as in the school, or through experiment, as in science, but through
> the dramatic depiction of action as a struggle to create and sustain
> order.[10]

Thus it is the function of art to engage the capacities of people to doubt and to endure the ambiguities of change.

> In art which is functioning as art, and not as a channel for official
> messages, [this capacity] even to revolt against the sacred principles
> of the social order, is not considered weak or treasonable, but heroic.
> We seek to open ends to reason in action. "The inquiry" of art is
> an inquiry over how to enact roles, not one "about" the reduction of
> roles to environmental factors, as in physical science, or over how
> to stifle doubt through faith, as in religion. The "argument" of
> art is a dramatic argument, and its persuasiveness lies in how it
> gives symbolic form to human relationships. Art does not teach us
> how to "think about" them but how to form roles so we can enact them
> in the social drama of community life.[11]

It will be my argument in this study that one can more adequately understand, judge, and appreciate the brief history of the West Side Organization if it is seen in these terms--as a testing of roles and relationships, as a public experiment with attitudes and conceptions of the real world, toward the end that a sense of the community and its purpose might be created and sustained.

CHAPTER II

THE SCENE AND THE ACTORS

WSO's Neighborhood

The Near West Side of the city of Chicago is an example of
urban real estate that has been the home for decades of some of the
poorest people of the city, but which now, in the seventh and
eighth decades of the twentieth century, is found to contain some
of the most valuable land in the entire urban area.

From the beginning the Near West Side was settled and re-
settled by those newer immigrants to the urban scene who had to
find a place to live near the rail yards, factories, and markets.
To this day it contains some of the oldest housing still in use in
the city.

Around the time of World War I, when the first black residents
arrived in the area they found housing that was already sixty and
seventy years old. Germans, Irish,and Scandanavians had been there
before them. Italians were still around and would retain a
pocket of their distinct community until the present. Greeks,
Poles,and Russian Jews would also be their neighbors for a time.
In more recent years, Latin groups have begun to settle on the
southern edges of the area. These later urban immigrants found
homes, not in new and planned housing developments, but in the
heavily used houses of their predecessors among Chicago's poor.

Eventually some of the worst of this housing was cleared away,
and The Chicago Housing Authority erected public housing projects.
The earliest of these "projects" were two- and three-story dwellings
which contrast strikingly with the later eight- and twelve-story
high-rise projects, the filing cabinet type buildings, which have
been the city's chief answer to the black housing problem. At the
time of this study a considerable proportion of the area's black
residents lived in the "projects" of the Near West Side, although
many others continued to live in the ancient single dwellings along
13th and 14th Streets, west of Ashland Avenue, and on some of the
side streets.

There is important Chicago history connected with the Near
West Side. Jane Addams' Hull House was built there, and its rem-
nant is maintained as a museum within the complex of ultramodern,
concrete structures of the Chicago Circle Campus of the University
of Illinois. Though the fabled enterprise has seen better days,
Chicago's flea market, the Maxwell Street open-air emporium, offered
its collection of bargaining, clipping, and fencing operations just
a few blocks from WSO headquarters.

But perhaps the most important history of the area has never
been written, and may never be, because the inner dynamics of
Chicago city politics are difficult, if not impossible, to record.

The Near West Side has a heavy political significance within the
city structures. It is part of Chicago's First Ward, the other
part of which is nothing less than the immensely valuable business
district, Chicago's Loop. The concrete canyons of the Loop contain
few resident voters, yet the First Ward elections of 1964 showed a
total vote of 20,890 in the race for Governor of Illinois. The
Loop is immensely valuable in economic terms for politically connected (or entangled) enterprises, such as insurance companies,
building services, food services, and food and liquor suppliers,
not to mention the real estate interests themselves. But at least
once every four years on ward election day, the political control
of the First Ward theoretically reverts to its franchised constituency.

In Chicago politics there has been no uncertainty regarding
the outcome in the First Ward for as long as anyone living there
remembers. The First Ward has been a controlled political entity.
The gubernatorial election of 1964 showed 82.3 percent of the
First Ward voting Democratic. Some of the men of WSO worked within
the regular Democratic organization in the ward in past years, and
they understood the resources of enforcement which were at its dis-
posal. This fact must be understood in order to understand further
why WSO's political behavior never involved a direct attack on the
political powers in the First Ward. WSO was involved directly in
some political campaigns, particularly in the Second Ward and the
former Second Congressional District, where figures who were independent of the regular party organization received WSO support for
alderman and the U.S. Congress. However, within the First Ward
itself WSO's political activity was confined to representing grievances from the people which the ward authorities could take care
of in the normal course of business. WSO's political agenda in
its home territory was to gain recognition from the political
powers of the First Ward of the needs and demands of the people
as these were represented by the leadership of WSO. WSO could push
hard for improvements which the ward authorities might grant or
respond to in the interests of "good government," but this form of
representation did not threaten the hard and fast political control
of the ward itself. The means to change the system of control were
never within WSO's resources and, apart from some instances of
harsh rhetoric about the "machine" and Mayor Daley, the discussion
of possible strategies for change was not part of the record of
WSO during years covered by this study.

The years have brought other changes which have made the land
itself on the Near West Side the kind of coveted territory that
can hardly be reserved indefinitely for the housing of the indigent
or the lower class. The Near West Side was bifurcated in the 1950s
by the huge east-west Eisenhower Expressway, which connects the
Loop with the Illinois Tollway at the farther reaches of Chicago's
western suburbs. WSO's immediate neighborhood was a corner of land
south of this expressway and west of the even newer north-south Dan
Ryan Expressway which was built along the western edge of the Loop
and reaches south to the outlying suburbs. This corner of territory
extends from the Eisenhower (about 800 South) to roughly 16th Street
South, where industrial property is concentrated. East to west, it
runs from the Dan Ryan (at about 700 West) to an indefinite line
shading off into the West Side proper at about Damen Avenue which
is 2000 West.

This portion of land thus described did not contain a homo-
genous population or a continuous residential community. There
were two white, middle class islands in the area, a new group of
residents living around the Chicago Circle Campus of the University,
and a small but vital Italian-American community occupying a two-
block-wide strip of land along Taylor Street, just two blocks north
of Roosevelt Road, the heartland of WSO. A huge tract of the
northern edge of territory along the Eisenhower is given over to
the West Side Medical Center of the University of Illinois and its
ancillary institutions, plus Cook County Hospital, Presbyterian-
St. Luke's Hospital, a Veterans Administration Hospital, industrial
clinics, student housing, a school for the blind, and the famous
Audy Home--the detention center for juvenile offenders of Cook
County. At the corner where the Dan Ryan and the Eisenhower expressways meet is the huge, new Chicago Circle Campus which en-
rolled more than 20,000 students within a few years of its erection
in the early sixties. The homes and businesses of the new Latin
residents run along Halsted Avenue south of Roosevelt Road (12th
Street South). The rest of the land contains the projects and
older homes of the black population of the Near West Side, including
the poorest of those whom WSO regarded as its constituency.
    The headquarters of the West Side Organization was located near
Ashland Avenue (1600 South) on the south side of Roosevelt Road. In
the years since the field work for the study was done, the entire
area north of Roosevelt Road and across the street from WSO has
been cleared, except for public housing that stands near Racine
Avenue. The south side of Roosevelt, from Ashland east to the
newest constructions belonging to the University of Illinois, has
the look of a condemned area, with decayed structures of wood and
plaster housing a few very poor families and many marginal businesses which could be wiped out in two days of energetic bulldozing.
    It is important to keep in mind that, though the larger area
of the Near West Side has immense facilities for human services and
education--the medical complex, the University, and several church
properties--the people of WSO felt, in 1964, that little if anything
of this was intended for them, or even available to them in their
desperate needs. Cook County Hospital, Audy Home, and the Cook
County Morgue were the exceptions. A large part of WSO's campaign
was to force the attention of these institutions to the needs of
the residents of the Near West Side, on the supposition that the
Illinois Medical Center and the University in particular, having
claimed so much of the land, and having been built with tax monies
which were collected from the poor as well as the upper and middle
classes, owed special responsibilities to the black poor who lived
nearby. There have been some genuine movements in this direction.
These have included employment opportunities at the University for
which WSO recommendees were hired, and better medical care for the
poor within the Illinois Medical Center.
    Beginning in 1964, WSO occupied a narrow storefront building
with a single room, perhaps sixty feet long and eighteen feet wide,
in the row of condemned structures along Roosevelt Road. The desks
of the officers (which used to be behind a partition that was removed early in the first year of WSO occupancy) were at the rear
of the room facing the door opening to the street. The furniture
was makeshift, including some pews, a small communion table obtained
from the former Cragin Congregational Church, and dilapidated

folding chairs placed in rows facing the front.   There was room for
about ninety people to be seated comfortably in a public meeting.
In 1966, the headquarters was decorated with signs and posters left
over from WSO street actions, clippings and pictures from news-
papers--including the city press as well as the *West Side Torch*
(WSO's publication)--which told of WSO activities and personalities,
numerous slogans and pictures of black leaders such as Martin
Luther King and Malcolm X, and some photographs of lynchings and
burnings in which white men and boys are shown standing around the
corpses of their black victims.   The room was depressing, certainly,
unless one was able to participate in the lively discussions and
hilarity that went on there.   The community meetings were held in
this room, usually on Wednesday night.   On occasion literally
hundreds of people packed the room to hear Martin Luther King or
Stokely Carmichael, or to engage in the discussion and decision-
making that occurred in time of crisis, such as the West Side riot
of 1966.

WSO's Leaders

Chester Robinson, WSO's first Executive Director, was a natural
leader whose style is not easy to comprehend according to familiar
prototypes.   At the time of this study, Robinson was in his mid-
thirties, heavy set, of average height.   He grew up in the neighborhood, and he continued to live there with his mother.   Robinson had
a record for narcotics violations which he acknowledged openly.
He had a warm and engaging manner that did not depend on pretense
of either the blusterly or self-effacing type.   He admitted to
being stubborn and cantankerous when he felt that way, and not at
all in possession of the graces of the middle class, an alleged
deficiency which he carried very lightly.   Taken from one of
Robinson's long, rambling, and often hilarious speeches before
WSO's community meeting, this example reveals some of these traits,

> I don't know what to say. Folks been talking about us like we was
> dogs. You don't pay no attention to that. They talked about Jesus
> Christ. He said, "Father, forgive them. They don't know what they're
> doing." I ain't goin to say that. I was reading in the paper that
> said we was violent and unstable. I'll go along with that last word.
> I *am* unstable. But they always criticize people when people start
> to stepping on their toes a little. You step on a man's toes and he
> wants to knock you down. That's a reaction. You never get a re-
> action like that from middle class folks. They always say, "I'm
> sorry," and things like that. I'm talking about folks like us. We
> don't do the same things other people do. So it don't bother me.

Robinson had a gift for expression which was pungent, appropriate, and unfailingly good humored.   In a community meeting he did
not preach or harangue, but he made his points with narrations
which were close to home in the experience of his listeners.

> The police told one of our members, "Man, what is you doing in that
> [WSO]. You're a fool for being in that organization. That organi-
> zation ain't no good. Give me one good reason why you're in WSO."
> The member answered, "Well, I'll tell you. I took sick, and my wife

is a mental patient. I been working on this job for a long time and
I had two weeks pay up there. The man fired me when I came out of
the hospital and I ain't got no food at home. Ain't got nothing. I
got babies at home." He might have been lying to me [Chester] when
he said he got down on his knees and asked the Lord which way to go.
But that is what he told me. And he was convincing. He said he
went first to the church, after the man told him he had to wait a
week for his check. He went to the preacher, who said, "You go back
again and maybe you can change his mind. I said, 'Why don't you go
with me'. The preacher said, 'That ain't my job'."

So he wandered around all that day. The next day he was walking
down Roosevelt Road and he looked up and saw that sign, WSO. He
said to himself, "I live on the West Side. Maybe that organization
will help me." So he came over to talk to me. Well, I was real
busy, and a lot of the time I'm real irritated. I'm going to be
frank about it. I asked him to talk to somebody else. He looked
like a drunken bum to me. But he was a man that was in trouble.
Not that I wouldn't have helped him. But I was busy talking with
somebody else.

So he went over and talked with Thirsty [Darden]. And when he was
through, Thirsty came over and talked with me. And then they talked
to Bob and Gene, and they said, "What do you mean, you can't get
your money. You worked for it. Let's go over there and see." They
went there to the Avenue and 15th Street, and in twenty minutes the
man had his check. And he told that to the police. And he said,
"As long as I live I'm going to belong to the West Side Organization!"

This is what counts. This is the whole thing that counts.

Robinson did not lose his reserve in public, probably reflecting a deep-seated instinct against being taken in by someone who
could manipulate others easily. His close friends were those he
had kept for long years. Critics described his style as that of a
ward politician, if not a petty political boss. More sympathetic
interpreters saw him adapting and elaborating a style of leadership
and communication learned in the streets.
As Director, most of Robinson's working time was spent at his
headquarters' desk. He kept in touch with affairs in the neighborhood by means of a constant stream of acquaintances and informants
who were in and out of the office. He used the Wednesday night
community meetings to sound his own opinions and beliefs, not expecting to be questioned or challenged in that forum.
A combination of openness, disarming frankness, and yet pro-
tectiveness, sometimes to the point of rigidity, made it difficult
to understand the real nature and depth of Robinson's commitments.
For instance, he understood genuine self-sacrifice to be a very
rare article which cannot be demonstrated in the short run. If he
was suspicious of good will and good intentions, of lofty ideals
and offers of assistance, it was because he suspected they clothed
a desire to control those to whom aid was being extended, that the
benefactor harbored a desire to be honored as a selfless humanitarian
and courageous fighter for the "underprivileged." At best, such
offers were made, he contended, by those who can well afford to
appear generous. To Robinson the long-term commitment was critical,

and not the particular ideology expressed. The goals that he stood
for were the bread and butter realities of daily life in the ghetto.
The scope of his concern was localized: "Nobody is gonna get me off
this corner."

Robinson was an "organization man" in style. As such, his
responses and actions were almost the opposite of those of a "movement" man, at least as imaged in the visions of a "movement among
the poor," which have been part of the ideology of much of the
freedom movement. Robinson insisted, again and again, that he was
not a violent man, but neither had he committed himself ahead of
time to courses of action that would be dictated by "philosophies"
(i.e., non-violence). Robinson helped to define the character and
style of WSO by standing against currents in "the movement" which
would have pulled WSO away from its local and practical involve-
ments. He acted to insure that the outcome of any struggle enhanced the welfare of WSO and its followers. He saw his interests
and those of the community as tied up with WSO. He helped to create
and to nurture an organization in the ghetto where none existed before, and involved many poor persons in it, most of whom had belonged to no other formal associations. In the public mind,
Robinson and WSO became identified, though this was by no means
true in WSO itself.

John Crawford was the youngest of the core of leaders, and
the one most often given the assignment of meeting outsiders and
presenting WSO to them. He was a large, powerfully built, young
man in his twenties, genuinely open and affable, hard working and
reliable. He was moved by deep religious feelings that gave a
quality of "soul" to his public addresses in the community meeting.
John was a preacher, though unordained and probably disinclined to
acknowledge the role. His "sermons," always spontaneous and about
sixty minutes long, were remarkable for the way scriptural imagery
was related to the situations ghetto people were facing. The
following quotation is offered as an example of Crawford's oratory
at its best. It was based on a "text" written on a blackboard in
the front of WSO headquarters, which read, "When the sho-nuff roll
in called, will your name be on the list?"

> Why, during the riots, were all kinds of people coming to WSO who
> hadn't been here before--priests, ministers, agency people, plus
> the youth and the people of the community? Why didn't they go to
> some church or other instead? The reason is there is a spirit here
> at WSO, a spirit of unity, a spirit that doesn't judge you because
> of what you have done, that looks upon a brother who is in bad
> shape through drunkenness, crime, etc., and says, "There but for
> the grace of God go I," a spirit that calls out from the echoes of
> your heart to communicate with the lost brother, to call you to
> responsibility, a spirit that goes through all kinds of changes in
> order to communicate with the brother whose name hasn't been called
> yet, to make sure that your name is on the role when it is called.
>
> To have a right to the tree of life, you must have responsibility.
> There must be communication and understanding. The names, like John
> Crawford, must be changed into flesh. The word must become flesh.
> Then the people will be moving. It won't be the Negroes moving,
> it will be the people moving. [Applause]

God is on the move. I believe that if you make one step, God is
going to make two. If God is on the move then we can go where we
want to go, because this is God's world. Some people say God is
dead. But people say God is dead because they are dead. [Applause]
There are three ways of being dead--mentally, spiritually, and
physically.

As Rev. Bevel said, I believe that I am God's son, and that I belong
everywhere that God is at home. When the prodigal son was lost in
corruption he didn't remember that he was the son of his father and
had a home where he belonged. But when he came to himself, he remembered and went to his father and was welcomed with open arms.
When we know we are God's sons, we know that our home is wherever
God is, and God is everywhere. So he is in Gage Park [white neigh-
borhood] and even in Cicero. Where God is, I belong, and can go.
As Jesus said, "In my Father's house are many mansions." And some
of those mansions may be in Gage Park. As sons of God we have the
responsibility to move because God is on the move.

WSO on Wednesday nights could seem to be a new kind of church
with its spirit of joy and hilarity mingled with the people's expressions of their hardship and near despondency. There were always a few present who were "floating high," but they were accepted
without resentment, and sometimes with good humor. It was Crawford
who interpreted the spirit of commitment and hope in WSO as creating
a religious community of a new kind for the people. To be sure,
the last thing that Crawford or any of the others wanted to have
was another storefront church in WSO, which may have been one reason
for the appeal in his presentation: that is, he was not a preacher
on the make for a congregation to support him and build his image
in the community.
    Crawford was at his best, however, in meeting with welfare
clients and attending to their grievances. He was the soul of
courtesy and understanding, a good listener, and responsive to
others. As one ADC mother said, "John always treats us with respect."
He was probably more unsure of himself in situations of tension and
anger. He deplored the strife and bickering that sometimes invaded
staff meetings and the day-to-day life at headquarters. He liked
things to be smooth and harmonious with everybody busy.
    William "Thirsty" Darden, a pensive and deliberate WSO leader,
entered WSO in the fall of 1964 with a request for help in having
his dishonorable discharge from the army reviewed, on the grounds
that his accusor was a white, Alabama non-com with whom he had had
a racially inspired altercation. He was convicted of insubordin-
ation. In his early thirties and a family man, he, like Crawford,
had a high school diploma, and gave evidence through independent
reading of strong intellectual interests. His leadership was
acknowledged when he was made Director of the Welfare Union. Darden
gained a reputation for being fearless in pursuing the claims of
welfare recipients until they received what was due them from the
Department of Public Aid. He communicated extremely well with
a small group because of his intensity and obvious dedication. He
was small and wiry but relished a confrontation wherein he could
show his mettle. Among friends he was warm and responsive; with
strangers he affected a cool distance that suggested one was being
tried in the balance and found wanting. He directed his attention

and charm where he determined and gave evidence of a sincerity that
was very persuasive. Respected by the men and women of WSO, young
and old alike, Darden had capacities of leadership that could en-
large his role in the years to come.
     Bill Clark became interested in WSO in the early days of the
Centennial dispute. From the beginning, WSO suited his style more
than any other organization he had ever encountered. Moreover, it
had interests and goals that struck a responsive chord. He was
expansive and flamboyant, with a reputation for physical prowess
and an uncertain temper that no one was anxious to test. He was
tall, handsome, gregarious, expressive, generous, and unpredictable.
Again, his commitments were not the kind that were evident on the
surface, but came through in surprising ways, usually at some crisis
point for WSO. He did a three-month jail term in 1966 for striking
a policeman during a battle that occurred at WSO in April of 1965.
The police had come, ostensibly to quiet a noisy crowd of teenagers
at a WSO dance. The shoving started--incited by the police, as WSO
later reported it in person to Chicago police chief, O. W. Wilson--
and Clark "intervened" to stop the beating of one boy. Clark's
troubles with the law were long-standing and serious enough that
he had to be careful.
     There were other WSO core people whose participation was con-
tinuous for a year or more, but who were never put on staff salaries.
In some ways, their commitments were all the more remarkable since
they gave faithful service when they were not employed or when they
had to carry jobs outside of WSO, though their real "vocation" was
with the organization. For now, they can be noted briefly: Earskin
Jones, a charter member and long time friend of Robinson's, an in-
valuable contact with the streets, and later advertising salesman
for the *West Side Torch*; Jimmy Halsell, once Chairman of the Community Council, later Secretary of the Board of Directors; Curtis
Beard, unemployed for over a year, keenly interested in the welfare
union work; Gene Harris, a cab driver who lost his job when he went
to Mississippi with Bill Darden during the voter registration march
of 1966, a fiery organizer and obviously devoted to the organization,
who stayed with WSO for over a year while his wife worked for the
family income; and Ralph Henry, an early participant in WSO activities, a contact man with civil rights and other movement groups in
the city.

Origins

     WSO grew from the mind of the Reverend Archibald Hargraves
who, in 1964, was Director of Mission Development for the Urban
Training Center for Christian Mission in Chicago. His idea was to
provide in WSO a ghetto base for Protestant ministers and seminary
students, mostly white men, inevitably middle class, who would undertake training to become involved with black men in the employment
issue.
     In form and intention WSO was envisioned by Hargraves as an
expression of Christian ministry in the modern city, a means for
enacting theological commitments reflecting the nature of authentic
Christian mission. This vision, together with the leadership and
money committed by the Urban Training Center to the founding of WSO,
represented motivations from sources outside the neighborhood scene.

How could predominantly white, middle class clergymen-trainees understand the experience of black men without jobs, without status and honor, without the economic power to affect their personal destiny in a productive society? The answer, of course, was that they could not identify with such experiences. Yet Hargraves proposed that the attempt be made to do so, by placing the trainees in an organization where the commitment of all, black and white, would be to accept the interpretation and the leadership of those who were experiencing this reality. The trainees were to attach themselves to an organization of the unemployed, joining the black men in their day-to-day confrontation with discrimination and joblessness in all of its meanings.

Such a group of black men, Hargraves believed, could be found in the informal associations of persons who knew and traveled with one another in the street society of the ghetto. In other words, Hargraves was determined *not* to tap the leadership of the formal organizations in the neighborhood, but to enlist men from the circles of friends and acquaintances who gathered in taverns, pool halls, barber shops, and other hospitable hangouts in the ghetto community, younger men just beyond the age of street corner gang societies.

Hargraves believed his vision and method challenged Saul Alinsky's philosophy of community organization. Alinsky's methods rely upon an infusion of money and trained organizational talent into a community to solidify existing organizational structures-- churches, agencies, businesses--by intensively organized compaigns, usually against an outside source of power which has an impact on the general community life, which was both highly visible and irritating. WSO, in Hargraves' vision, was to reveal what could be done in another way. The poor themselves, and the leaders they would offer would define the issues and direct the action.

The first task was to find the natural leaders in the street associations and to channel their energies toward improving their own lot and that of their fellows, those closest to them in spirit and circumstance. Then the base would be provided where the middle class trainees could gain first hand experience of the difficulties and the possibilities of joint action with the poor.

The organizational effort began with a one-to-one style of recruitment. Hargraves had contacts in the community from the days in the early 1950s when he helped found and lead a Protestant parish on Roosevelt Road patterned after the successful experimental community in New York City called the East Harlem Protestant Parish. Unemployed men were contacted by these friends and asked to a meeting in a storefront church on Roosevelt Road, Holy Trinity, which was part of the original parish organization Hargraves had founded.

Three men showed up and Hargraves explained his purpose. He and some other ministers who were present with him were offering to join the unemployed men in an effort to be directed by the local men themselves. Together they would face the problems of no jobs, no income. Hargraves offered several examples for their consideration of how the effort might begin. Perhaps they could organize rent strikes in slum buildings, withholding the rent money from the landlord and with that money hire the unemployed tradesmen from the community to fix up the building. Another tactic might be to start a small business, using the skills of the men present. The men could help one another, and others as well, to develop some new

skills. He then asked each of the men to share with the group the
difficulties that they faced in looking for, or in keeping employment. One man reported that he had lost a steady job when his boss
moved to Tennessee. Another said he could not afford to commute to
a suburb, where the firm he had worked for had transferred. The
last man had undertaken training with a public service agency, but
had received no job on completing the training. They told of others
they knew who had been hired, required to pay union initiation fees,
and then fired just before their qualifying period ended, at which
time the union could have protected their jobs.

Three days later one of the men at the meeting, Blutcher
Bryant, went with one of the UTC staff members, Donald Keating, to
a local barbershop where they found Chester Robinson, a licensed
barber, then out of work. The Reverend Chris Gamwell of Trinity
Church knew Robinson, who had taught black history in the church's
storefront. Robinson heard some of the ideas propounded at the
first meeting, and then contributed his own. Why not, he suggested,
organize the unemployed in the community to protest against a local
business on grounds of discrimination in its hiring practices?
(This was, of course, several years before Operation Breadbasket
had instituted boycotts against chain food stores on this ground.)
Robinson mentioned Centennial Laundry, a large firm on Roosevelt
Avenue, which employed many black persons at menial jobs inside the
plant, but none in its management or customer sales services. Centennial, he felt, would be a good target for action.

Another meeting at Trinity Church a few days later brought into
the group John Crawford, who had a long and frustrating story of
personal difficulties with the Department of Public Aid and its job
training programs. In this way the founding core of WSO was re-
cruited.

The roots of WSO were also in the reality of "the Movement,"
by which is meant the coming together of people from various sectors
of black community life in America (joining with committed whites in
many instances) for the purpose of enacting a sense of freedom and
right in relation to a multitude of offenses suffered by the members
of an American lower caste.

As suggested above, the content of movement ideology as expressed in WSO is one major concern of this study, as WSO was one
of the earliest attempts to tap the sensitivities of urban blacks,
the unemployed males--especially the street-wise leadership--for
their understanding of the predicaments and desires of the ghetto
poor. Two years before "Black Power" became a diffuse ideological
symbol for a host of movement causes and groups, WSO leaders articulated clearly a number of grievances, imperatives, and prerogatives
which express the theme of self-determination for the ghetto people
in those areas which affect their lives directly--particularly
employment, welfare, and police power. It is important to know that
these early expressions of the meaning of "Black Power" did not
build consciously upon now familiar attempts to fill that symbol
with meaning. WSO would have been a different sort of organization
if, instead of beginning in 1964, it had begun its program in the
summer of 1966, when Stokely Carmichael and others first penetrated
the news media with their theme of "Black Power."

The financial commitment of the Urban Training Center to WSO
in the early months was confined to the salaries of two consultants,
Don Keating and Robert Strom, both committed white clergymen with

experience in community organization in other urban settings.   In
addition, stipends were given to students assigned to the organization for various periods of training.   Soon it became obvious that
in order to have an organization, an indigenous staff would have to
be supported by outside funds until other resources, preferably
within the community, could be found.   A sum of $9,000 from the
Urban Training Center was devoted to this purpose and to the rental
of a separate headquarters for WSO.
     The role of outsiders, the Urban Training Center consultants,
was declared to be that of participants supporting the efforts of
the unemployed in tackling their problems of finding meaningful
employment.   At the first meeting of men contacted on the streets,
on June 26, 1964, in the parish storefront of Holy Trinity Church,
Keating expressed this strategy:

> We all loath the idea of coming here to run an organization for full
> employment. We are here to see if we can support you in organizing
> to do something about jobs. And we are beginning in this way--trying
> to come to where you are and letting our commitment to each other
> determine where we go from here.

This was the ideological baptism of what became the West Side Organization.
     To the West Side Organization the members brought their own
resources of leadership learned in the streets, obtained through
lifetimes of confronting personal and social problems from positions
of relative powerlessness.   They contributed their essential perspective upon the celebrated problems of the unemployed black male,
of his family and dependents, caught within a cycle of victimization.
Moreover, they brought into the organization the spirit of rejuve-
nated American blacks, participating in a movement which was, in
the years 1964-66, just beginning to identify and to express the
resources of Black Power.
     The West Side Organization was created explicitly to allow an
organization to form, a program and leadership to develop, *in the
style* of the people who are the poorest residents of a West Side
ghetto.
     Kenneth Burke defines the essence of style as "ingratiation,"
the " . . . attempt to gain favor by the hypnotic or suggestive
process of 'saying the right thing'."   WSO was intended to become
a representative organization, a community power, by saying and
doing the "right thing" on behalf of the desperately poor of their
neighborhood.   It will be my argument in this study that WSO's
strategy for gaining representative authority and legitimation was
fundamentally that of "ingratiation."
     The WSO story is an instance of a group of leaders acting
consciously as "representative" of a people "who are just like us,"
who are "in the same shape as we are."   Actually, WSO had no other
means at hand for building its constituency and gaining bargaining
power for the people than that of "saying the right thing," and
saying it often by *doing* the thing which would be recognized as in
the interest of those it considered to be the "real" people of the
ghetto.   The real financial or political capital with which WSO
began was incredibly small.   Nothing *could* happen unless, in some
way, the group could gain and feel the support of the people to whom
it appealed.   The story reveals, I believe, the nature and extent

of that support in WSO's community. It never became the massive
manifestation of "movement" that its founders and leaders hoped it
would. Yet, there is sound evidence that WSO achieved, for a brief
time, a type of legitimation which, in that period, was unique
among black community groups. WSO's impact upon sectors of the
city, particularly the public media, the welfare system, the police,
and certain groups within the business and ecclesiastical community
was greater than anyone would have predicted who knew only WSO's
financial and organizational limitations.

CHAPTER III

CENTENNIAL LAUNDRY:
CONFRONTING THE IDEOLOGY OF
EXCLUSION

The Target

When Chester Robinson was invited to respond to the idea of
forming an action group of black men to work on problems of employment, his immediate reply was to identify the Centennial Laundry as
a target within the community which represented the employment problems of black men. Although Centennial employed mostly blacks
within its large Roosevelt Road plants, it did not employ them at
a standard of pay on which they could do more than subsist in a low
economic status. Nor could they hope to rise to a level of dignified
responsibility within the company. This was Robinson's perception
of the problem, and it quickly won acceptance among the small group
of men that were coming together initially under Hargraves' leadership.

Robert Strom and Blutcher Bryant paid a visit to the laundry
plant on August 12, 1964. This was actually the third time WSO had
called there. On an earlier visit Donald Keating, a white man, had
asked routine questions of the management and had received what he
recorded as an encouraging response from the owner--an agreement
to cooperate in a program of aiding the unemployed on the West Side.
However, on an even earlier call, Blutcher Bryant, a local black
man, had been rebuffed by the plant manager. Chester Robinson reported knowing a number of people who had begun work at the laundry
at $1.04 per hour, and had risen to $1.19 per hour after four years.
Centennial was already under suspicion within WSO as an exploiter
of black labor when Strom and Bryant met with the plant manager on
that summer day.

Strom's written report dwelt upon the alleged degradation of
the black workers within the plant. The black men and women were
said to be treated by their white bosses in a servile fashion; they
were routinely called by their first names, or referred to as "boy,"
or the circumstances of their private lives were exposed to the
strangers by the manager. One woman was presented to Strom and
Bryant in this way: "This is Millie; her husband is a bum and she
needs this job. Right Millie?" The visitors were told that individuals who went on weekend drunks were kept on as long as they be-
haved themselves during four days of the week. Members of families
were hired as favors to those already employed at Centennial. Small
loans and other favors provided by the management engendered the
dependency of the employees. Lie detector tests were required of
workers suspected of being responsible for the loss of garments.
Double time cards allegedly were used to permit payment of overtime
work on straight-time rates. Neighborhood children were hired for

a few cents daily to ride laundry trucks in the black neighborhood.
There were no grievance procedures except through the owner, or
through other members of his family who were employed at high management positions.

Bryant raised with the plant manager the question of black
route drivers on Centennial's trucks. Of thirty-two routes driven
by Centennial's employees, at least eight were in the black community itself. A good route driver could earn three and even four
times the amount paid to laborers inside the laundry plant. Furthermore, it was the driver who represented the company in its face-to-
face dealing with the public. With the route trucks came responsibility for large daily cash transactions and visibility as a trusted
man in a real business enterprise.

The issue provoked a heated discussion between the two men.
The manager admitted that not one of Centennial's drivers was a
black man, nor had there ever been a black man driving for the firm.
According to Strom, his reasons were that no *qualified* black drivers
had ever presented themselves for one of these jobs, but if one
ever did, the company could not hire him because of the unwillingness of the heads of families to allow their wives to have direct
dealings at their doors with black men. Black men were largely
unfit to do a job which untrained white men do, and they could not
be trusted with white women, or at least the white man's belief
that they could not be trusted had to be respected. Such were the
"classic" explanations for Centennial's employment record through
more than forty years of doing business in a black neighborhood.

The next step for WSO was to leaflet the community announcing
public "hearings" on Centennial's employment policies. These were
held on subsequent Wednesday nights in a setting resembling, in
some details, a storefront church meeting. Songs were sung--not
gospel, but freedom songs. Testimonies were heard--not of "spiritual"
transformations, but of the "victories" WSO had wrought in finding
jobs or dealing with problems brought through its doors. Orations
were delivered by one of the leaders, or sometimes by several.
Announcements of events sponsored, or approved of, by WSO were
given. And a kind of altar call was issued for people willing and
ready to "get committed" to WSO and its program.

In addition to the enthusiasm and rallying, WSO now introduced
an opportunity for people to speak up regarding their grievances
with Centennial Laundry. A number of these spoken complaints portray the victimization suffered by people who have only their labor
and occasionally modest skills to use in bargaining with employers.
None of those who spoke knew of any advocates of their position who
could be counted upon to pursue their rights and their needs. This
was true even though everyone who had worked with Centennial's
operation was forced to belong to a union and contribute to it out
of his or her meagre earnings.

Responses

This sudden activity on the part of a few local black men and
their white allies against a long established West Side enterprise
provoked instantaneous and uniform responses. To counteract the
militants, it was supposed one must get to their leadership, i.e.,
the most vocal white man, Strom. The owner and the plant manager
of the laundry were the first to react. The day after notices
were peddled throughout the community announcing a public meeting
to discuss Centennial's hiring policies, the two men came to WSO
and demanded to speak to Strom. They were informed that he, in

fact, did *not* speak for WSO. There was an angry exchange and the
Centennial people left.

Within a few days WSO received word from the Chicago City
Missionary Society that certain of its prominent executive committee members, men high in the management of industrial and utility
corporations downtown, had been called by the owner of Centennial
Laundry. Informed of what their employee, Bob Strom, was doing with
a following of black residents of the Near West Side, the threat
was direct--call off Strom, or face a suit brought by the laundry.
Strom and Keating were called to a meeting of executive committee
members to explain what was happening. Here, and on many subsequent
occasions, the two consultants made their chief point--that it was
wrong for them to be speaking for the cadre. The entire WSO project
was devoted to finding and enabling leadership to emerge from among
the men on the streets, who must be allowed to state WSO's position.

Another meeting was arranged wherein Bryant and Robinson spoke
for the first time to the men of power in urban society. The result
of that meeting was that the leadership of CCMS was drawn into the
struggle. The meeting did not end the attempt of certain members
of the executive committee to extricate themselves and their employed
staff, Strom and Keating, from WSO and its activities, but the
chairman and his closest associates were, from this point on, unwilling to slip out of the controversial experiment in this way.
The key leaders were intrigued by the project of fostering these
new expressions of leadership on the Near West Side, although they
were necessarily restive about the structures of accountability
that could be established between WSO and the institutions they
represented.

The WSO leadership, for its part, was skeptical of their motives,
questioning whether there could be interest and commitment of funds,
political influence, prestige, and energy without the existence
also of the subtle desire to control. Yet the cadremen were also
anxious to enhance the public significance of WSO through contact
with these groups, and they obviously needed their financial support
to carry the program forward. The task for WSO was how to be truly
independent, though bound with influential and powerful people in
Chicago. The task for CCMS was to keep a majority of the Board
with the leadership and avoid losing the opportunity to help WSO.

The cadremen relied upon the commitments of Keating and Strom
to submit themselves to the discipline of the organization in its
decision-making process. The two white consultants were caught between the board of CCMS, with its power to cut off funds and withdraw its staff employees from the action on the Near West Side, and
the organization they sought to serve.

From time to time signals were received from "downtown" about
the Board's difficulties in justifying its continued support for
WSO in its direct action campaign against a legitimate business
operation. There were various attempts to set the limits beyond
which CCMS support could not venture. Picketing in front of the
laundry itself was one such highly sensitive issue. There were
attempts to require Keating and Strom to urge the organization to
cease this activity before suit was brought against CCMS, but Keating
argued that the decision had been made by the cadre and ratified
within the community meeting, and their only choice was to stick it
out or leave the scene. The early records of WSO's first year,
meticulously kept by Don Keating in the form of a daily "log,"

reveal no instances of wavering on the essential point--leadership belonged within the community, and the outsiders could participate on that basis only. CCMS chose to stay in until they were eventually bound by a civil suit. Then, in a startling reversal, it became the task of the people downtown to prove the *independence* of the cadre from any influence and direction from the Society.

The fuller story of WSO's courtship and persuasion of its white liberal "constituency" will be developed in relation to the responses WSO made to a direct challenge from the black militant left, and in relation to the various attempts at mediation between the adversaries in the laundry dispute.

In the meantime, another challenge to the leadership had been received at WSO headquarters, this time from a prominent and politically connected black minister in the Lawndale area several miles west of WSO, who announced that he had been asked by the Centennial management to intervene in the dispute. He asked to meet with Bob Strom (again) in his church office to try to get to the bottom of the dispute. Blutcher Bryant, John Crawford, and Bob Strom met with the minister-spokesman.

This encounter produced very little beyond a clear indication that Centennial was greatly exercised over an impending direct action and was prepared to use pressures and threats of various kinds. The minister let it be known that both he and the Centennial management were well connected politically, and WSO could expect difficulties in relation to the police and/or other public agencies in any attempt it might make to gain a legal status as a bargaining agent. Nevertheless, he said, Centennial was prepared to be reasonable and had indicated a willingness to begin training two black men for the route jobs in exchange for an end to harassment by WSO. Furthermore, he was empowered to act as negotiator with the organization. The WSO representatives took this information back to the staff meeting. Immediately thereafter the minister was informed that his services as mediator and negotiator were rejected. WSO's public meetings would go on as scheduled.

Shortly thereafter WSO was visited by a succession of building and electrical inspectors from the city, plus a delegation of police who were checking on WSO's policies as an employment-finding agency. When the police left WSO's premises they were observed entering the Centennial plant down the street. A call to the district police headquarters revealed no record on an investigation ordered or reported by its officers. WSO suspected that the police were sent into WSO on orders from someone outside the normal chain of command. All of this meant to the cadremen that they had struck a sensitive nerve in the Centennial operation and that they had every reason to continue.

Negotiations

At a public meeting WSO's position was formally adopted. The original demands were as follows:

1. Eight routemen were to be hired immediately by Centennial.
2. The black minister was to be rejected as a mediator.
3. The owner of Centennial was asked to meet with the people of WSO at the next community meeting.

By the next meeting the owner of the laundry had rejected *all* demands and made calls to the employers of Bob Strom. WSO then took the following further actions:

1. Negotiations with Centennial were to continue.
2. The neighborhood was to be organized for possible direct action.
3. A plan was to be worked out for a selective patronage campaign.

But before the next scheduled community meeting on September 2, the adversary had changed from a lion to an agreeable puppy. The owner, through his attorney, proposed an agreement with WSO in which the following proposals were made:

1. Two black routemen would be hired immediately and paid $80 per week while training.
2. More black routemen would be taken on as positions became available, with WSO recommendees given preference when they qualified.
3. No WSO recommendee would be fired from Centennial without first consulting WSO, and his successor would also be taken from WSO's recommendees.
4. WSO could discuss Centennial's labor policies at any time, including any matters not specifically restricted to labor/management relations.
5. Centennial would take on a WSO man immediately if he were able to show, experience as a presser.
6. The Centennial management would join a West Side employer's council to work with WSO.

The reaction in WSO ranged from elation to, "It's just too good to be true." At the next community meeting Centennial's offer was accepted as something to be given a trial. It seemed as if the Centennial conflict might end then and there.

In a few short weeks, however, WSO perceived that the agreement was a hollow one. WSO recommendees had not been hired, having been found unsuitable according to Centennial's standards. Moreover, a white man had been recently taken on as a driver when he quit his route job with another laundry. One black man had been taken into training as a routeman, but he was the son of another employee. So WSO announced the resumption of its campaign against Centennial, reiterating its original demands for eight route jobs and for Centennial to conduct its hiring business within WSO's office.

Internal Dynamics

At this point there was tension in the staff over WSO having been taken in by Centennial. Robinson declared that he had been skeptical about the laundry's proposed settlement from the start, but he had gone along with the white consultants, who had responded naively to Centennial's "trickelation." Moreover, he had received information that the abortive agreement had been engineered from "downtown," i.e., through intervention from the higher-ups of the Chicago City Missionary Society Board--WSO's allies. In exchange

for the promise to rein in their obstreperous employee, Bob Strom,
Centennial had promised CCMS to make the accessions described in
the proposal. It is not clear from Keating's notes how this charge
was verified, if it ever was. But it became accepted as truth within WSO and was never denied by the Chicago City Missionary Society.

The issue shifted quickly from the assignment of blame over
who had precipitated the premature accession to Centennial's "agreement," to the nature of the strategy itself. This became a point
of testing the goals WSO ought to pursue and the methods it should
use in the Centennial action project. Not surprisingly, it was a
testing of the local, black leadership against the outside, white
leadership within WSO.

In the early weeks of the action program at WSO several white
activists had been drawn into the WSO cause. Two of them in particular, Lee Webb and Clayton Hewett, were seasoned veterans of
community organization and activism. They had argued, in the early
staff meetings, that the scope of WSO's grievances against Centennial
should not be so narrow as to concentrate upon a few driver's positions. Centennial was only one of several large laundry operations
in the inner city that ought to be attacked. It represented a
system wherein large service institutions lived off the cheap labor
and patronage of the residents but gave nothing substantial in
return. The strategy of WSO should be directed, they said, not to
obtaining a few higher paying positions but toward instigating a
wide public response against the total injustice of the situation.
Moreover, tactically speaking, Centennial provided WSO with an excellent organizing issue. The last thing WSO should hope for was
a victory it would win at the expense of Centennial. The more Centennial resisted, the more it could be portrayed as the representative of an evil system which had to be changed, and the more WSO's
prominence as an organizing force could be enhanced.

Against this argument Chester Robinson was adamant. In fact,
the issue provoked a near break in the unity of the staff when,
during one such discussion, Robinson stalked out of the meeting in
high anger and was only later retrieved through Strom's inter-
cessions. Robinson's points were as follows:

1. He knew that the interest of *the community* was not upon
    large issues of corruption or exploitation, but upon the
    one "bread and butter" issue of whether *real* jobs were
    going to be open to local men; Hewett, Webb, *et al.* simply
    did not understand the West Side community.

2. There was reason behind the management of Centennial
    attempting to get WSO concerned about the whole plant as
    an issue. The union for plant workers was, he alleged, a
    company union with crime syndicate connections. If WSO
    were to take on the union directly, the syndicate could
    take care of the trouble-makers. Robinson believed this
    to be, in fact, Centennial's strategy, because he had
    identified certain people who were making these exact
    suggestions at the open meetings as spies from Centennial
    itself.

3. The people actually working within Centennial were not
    blacks from the Near West Side, but Uncle Toms. In other

words, they were not the "real" people WSO represented or should try to help.

It is hard to assess the various points Robinson was making in this instance. There is no question that some of them were simple rhetorical strategies to put off the suggestions of outsiders with whom he disagreed. Robinson could "know" what concerned the "real" people, and the white consultants could not.

In any case, Robinson's argument was accepted, and the broader, Alinsky-style, method of organization around an issue provided by the antagonist himself was not to become WSO's strategy. The same contention appeared again in community meetings and in other strategy consultations; why should WSO be concerned with high paying jobs for a very few while the masses suffer? But the staff united thereafter on that point. WSO was not after improvements within the plant operation for their own people but the breaking of a pattern which was felt as oppressive.

That oppressiveness included the standards of qualification by which Centennial claimed to be a "fair opportunity employment" firm, standards which effectively excluded the black men of the ghetto. Centennial required, among other things, that its drivers be bondable with no criminal record, that they have a continuous and satisfactory employment record (no gaps), and that they be living within the bonds of respectable marriage. Further, they were required to "pass" a lie detector test on the facts that appeared in their employment applications. "Fulfill all of these requirements," said Centennial, "and your race will provide no barrier to your employment."

Though there certainly are young men in the ghettos who could fulfill all of these requirements, they apparently had never presented themselves to Centennial Laundry for the job of routeman. More to the point, these were not the men for whom WSO sought to speak and to act. The man educated in the streets of the West Side could never meet Centennial's standards, if only because a perfect record with the police is very hard to maintain for a boy who has not been kept indoors all of his life. Moreover, the prerequisite of experience and a good employment record functioned as a vicious cycle to prevent willing workers from gaining experience and maintaining continuous employment. In short, Centennial's fair employment policy was an act of "trickelation" by which able-bodied men, capable of driving a truck, managing simple cash transactions, and restraining their lust at the sight of a housewife in curlers, were blocked out of gainful employment in their own community because they were black.

This accounts for the second major demand which WSO sought to impress upon Centennial in addition to the hiring of black routemen. It was to allow WSO to decide *who* was qualified to drive for the laundry. WSO would select and recommend applicants, and Centennial was expected to impose no further hurdles to their employment, but to give them a chance when an opening occurred.

This would seem an outrageous demand for a community organization, or even a union, to make, *except* in situations where a firm can hire only union approved apprentices. WSO was asking, in effect, to perform this function for the laundry--to stake its reputation as a responsible community organization on finding and qualifying men for the work at Centennial. Of course, WSO had no reputation

yet to defend, but it was intent on forcing Centennial to make an
important accession to black leadership in the ghetto, namely, that
it was capable of determining the fitness of a candidate for a job
in exactly those areas in which white management was incapable,
i.e., in positions where factors of character and culture are de-
cisive, rather than a minimal skill.

Boycott

Following the failure of the agreement with Centennial Laundry,
in the early part of October 1964, WSO began its most intensive
period of activism against the laundry. Centennial's management
was accused of reneging on its agreement to hire black routemen and
to accept WSO's recommendees. This was interpreted as an agreement
with the "community," and the neighborhood was canvassed for persons
willing to carry signs in front of the laundry plant on Roosevelt
Road. A post-picketing meeting was scheduled each day to talk over
the day's events and plan for the next. In later months this period
of activism was interpreted by Crawford and others as a high point
for WSO's life, although Keating's records indicate numerous minor
difficulties with the staff over the assignments and responsibilities
connected with the action. But new persons were coming into WSO
who were willing to picket Centennial. The news media had taken
notice of this controversial new approach to the problems of employment within a community. Centennial indicated that it had been
hurt by the action campaign against its business by pressuring
WSO's "downtown" allies, and by threatening suit on the grounds that
the laundry had actually hired a black driver as a trainee and WSO
had been unable to send qualified applicants. Robinson and others
were certain that "spies" from the laundry were always present within WSO's community meetings.
        The period of exhilaration in WSO over its activism and re-
sponse was short-lived due to a court injunction against the picketing of Centennial obtained by the laundry management. This injunction was considered dubious on constitutional grounds and drew
the attention of civil libertarian lawyers, but its effect was to
stifle WSO activism at the height of its success.

A Militant Challenge

WSO was now forced to deal with another sort of challenge to
its leadership in the community, this time from representatives of
an ideologically militant group on the West Side. On October 21,
representatives from a group called ACT came to the WSO community
meeting and engaged in a lively debate on the question of arming
the people who were picketing in front of Centennial. These representatives came, they said, as a response to WSO's invitation to
civil rights organizations in Chicago to join them in their program
of action. ACT was the only group to respond.
        The debate that evening was long and often incoherent. The
ACT people were eager to drive home their position that non-violence
was a weak tactic unless it contained the explicit threat of retaliation by force to force. The leader of ACT made the point ex-
plicitly:

If an ACT picketer is molested I guarantee the aggressor will be killed. Freedom is death and death is freedom.

Chester Robinson attempted to parry this stirring challenge in an emotionally alive public meeting:

This is a young organization. We are not familiar with picketing. I think most of the male members [of WSO] are not like the usual members of the middle class civil rights groups. We don't understand "turning the other cheek." We have never lived by it. But the question is: Is it right? We don't want to start anything. People in this area do not like Centennial Laundry. We don't want to start a riot.

Another cadreman, Jimmy Halsell, added the following to the debate:

This is a community organization. We don't want to say violence. This is all that we know around here. Life here is violence. We want to hold our heads up. We want to be citizens living within the law. We want to be constructive. If we organize this community we will win at Centennial Laundry. Everyone has to be ready for violence. That's it.

It would seem that the debate was never drawn in such a way that a clear disagreement on violence versus non-violence was articulated. WSO leaders equivocated but showed nonetheless that the community could not affirm ACT's ideology of armed defense. The meeting was long and included a charge from ACT that WSO was unable to move because it included white men at the top level of leadership. On the next day, the ACT representative called the owner of Centennial Laundry and announced ACT's intention of joining WSO in its picketing. This prompted a series of panic calls to CCMS and a relay to WSO, with the direct ultimatum from CCMS, "If you go with ACT, you go without CCMS." WSO met in staff session to discuss the issues. Bob Strom tried to line out the alternatives clearly, with an indication that a decision was required. WSO could go the route of revolution and align itself with the ACT militants. They, and others, would be happy to have WSO's access to the people on the Near West Side. Or WSO could try to stick with their allies in the power structure and use their influence to make WSO's interpretations of the problems felt. There was no hesitation on the part of WSO's leadership. ACT had been fended off the night before when its people had attempted to sway the public meeting. WSO's direction would be to make the power structure hear and respond to its perceptions of social reality. It was decided that the ACT people must be called off the picket lines, and that was done. This decision had a very positive effect upon the leading members of the CCMS Board who had been feeling a great deal of pressure from their constituency in the churches to pull away from WSO and its style of activism which was upsetting to a business-oriented membership. However, the threat of anarchy which seemed implicit in the ideology of the emerging militants was feared even more. The local leadership of WSO held off this threat in the midst of a volatile public encounter. The next day it took explicit actions which denied to the ACT leaders an entrance to the activist campaign.

CCMS leaders identified this as the mark of real leadership emerging among the people, which they could interpret to their troubled constituencies. Militancy in the cause of economic justice for unemployed blacks who faced exclusion from meaningful employment could be distinguished from the threat of violence in the streets.

The result was that much of the pressure within the Board against WSO, which had taken the explicit form of pressure to shed Strom, Keating, and its other entanglements with WSO was alleviated. Instead CCMS asked that clear lines of communication between the community organization and the Society be maintained so that the Board could do its proper job of interpretation. WSO need not feel obliged to "clear with downtown" before taking action, but it must undertake the responsibility of providing accurate information.

The response within WSO to this definition of its relationship and responsibilities to CCMS is illuminating. Robinson saw this minimal request for accurate and up-to-date information as a way for the leadership of CCMS to retain a piece of the action. There was a fine line between mutual interest, mutual responsibilities, and the attempt to control. Robinson would remain skeptical, yet he was aware also that WSO had achieved a position of respect.

Further Negotiations and an Injunction

During the first phase of WSO's public action against Centennial the CCMS Board had indeed infused its own interests and conceptions of the conflict by introducing agents of mediation. First, the Fair Employment Practices Commission and later, the Chicago Commission on Human Relations attempted to investigate the dispute and intervene between the community organization and the laundry. In both cases their actions seemed to have been instigated by requests from CCMS Board members who were obviously hoping to end the matter.

These initiatives were not particularly welcome to WSO; nor were they rebuffed. WSO maintained that it had nothing to hide and was willing to consider whatever might be forthcoming from the attempts of these groups to mediate. WSO maintained, of course, that the dispute was between the laundry and the "community," and decisions would have to be submitted to the community meetings. Meanwhile, the leadership of WSO would listen and consider.

The actual process of negotiation and mediation is a long and very complicated story. Eventually, the Commission on Human Relations played the larger role in trying to establish some agreements. This phase of the activity, which lasted for more than one month in the fall of 1964, brought WSO into fuller contact with sympathetic, white liberal forces in several areas of the city's public life.

The negotiating process came to a climax on October 28 when a letter from Centennial Laundry was received at WSO headquarters which was supposed to contain an agreement worked out between the disputants by the Chicago Commission on Human Relations. The letter was, in fact, a statement of "general principles" upon which the management and WSO were allegedly in agreement, including a reference to "the brotherhood of man and the fatherhood of God." The hard specifics, hammered out verbally in the negotiating process which Edward Marciniac from CCHR had sponsored, were simply left out. WSO had a community meeting scheduled for that night, and it was agreed

to allow the Centennial lawyer to read the letter in the meeting
and then to compare it with the details of the verbal agreement,
as they had been recorded by a CCHR negotiator, who would also be
at the public meeting, and who could attest to the "betrayal." The
public meeting came off as planned. Chester Robinson spelled out
WSO's understanding of the substance of the agreement, and the CCHR
man concurred. The lawyer argued that Centennial's commitment was
to the larger principles involved, and he pleaded for trust on the
basis of his own liberal record as a champion of the civil rights
of the oppressed. He was, in fact, hooted down in the meeting.

WSO reverted immediately to its tactics of picketing and door-
to-door appeals to boycott Centennial. The management responded
with the successful plea in the District Court of Illinois for an
injunction against WSO's campaign of activism. On November 12, 1964,
the subpoenas were received by all of the cadremen, Strom, Keating,
and Hargraves, and numerous members of the CCMS Board. The charges
listed many others, including fifty John Does intended to include
any members of WSO not specifically named. The injunction sought
was actually tied to a civil suit against WSO and CCMS brought by
Centennial in which it charged loss of business and good will, plus
personal damages, all amounting to $500,000.

The injunction, if allowed to stand, would have throttled the
first major effort which WSO had launched, by which it had gained
attention throughout the city and had been able to rally significant
numbers of West Siders to its banner. It hit WSO at its highest
point of activity and public support. It also tied WSO irrevocably
with the CCMS leaders downtown, since Don Benedict was named in the
suit as the "founder" of WSO. In short, there was a great deal at
stake for everyone concerned in the attempt to halt WSO in its
tracks.

The first reaction within WSO leadership was exultation, in
the belief that WSO had finally brought Centennial out into an open
fight where, it was assumed, the laundry would be revealed for what
it was--an exploiter of black people--and WSO's activism would be
sustained. But the proceedings in the District Court the next day
showed the reality to be otherwise. Abner Mikva was retained by
CCMS to fight the injunction on behalf of all parties involved.
He asked that the request for an injunction be transferred to a
Federal Court. On the afternoon of November 13, Judge Julius
Hoffman heard the arguments in Federal Court and remanded the entire
matter back to the District Court, where the injunction was granted.
WSO now had to deal with the issue of whether its commitment to law-
ful obedience included a willingness to be stymied by the courts.

The cadremen were incensed by the action of the court. There
was much talk of defying the injunction and continuing the picketing
of the laundry. However, Robinson and Bryant were favorably im-
pressed with Mikva's advocacy, and they accepted his interpretation
of the injunction as a very serious matter which affected civil
liberties of the most basic sort. Mikva believed the injunction
to be unconstitutional on the grounds that it infringed the right
of free speech through peaceful demonstrations. He interpreted the
injunction to mean that WSO was temporarily enjoined against direct
actions involving the persons and property of Centennial, but that
it did not prevent them from actions by which WSO could interpret
their situation in general to its constituency and maintain the

loyalty of the people throughout the attempt to have the injunction removed.

WSO had previously scheduled a street rally for the Saturday following the injunction, and this was translated into a public gathering held away from the Centennial buildings in which the injunction could be explained to the people and the WSO cause affirmed. The rally was held with Hargraves in the role of interpreter. He urged the people to be scrupulous in obeying the letter of the injunction but not to lose confidence in the forces seeking to preserve their rights to free speech, especially WSO. The injunction was, in fact, so broad that the leadership of WSO was effectively stopped for fear of endangering their personal liberty. The cadremen had records with the courts which might result in severe penalties if they were arrested for defying the courts.

More than a year passed before the civil suit was tried and lost by Centennial. But by then WSO had moved on into other fields of activity. Nevertheless, the court's decision was marked in WSO as a "victory" for the organization and the community.

Autonomy

In the meantime, the crisis for WSO had become internal. The initial funding of the organization from the Urban Training Center was expended and not renewed, the UTC board having decided that it was not funded to provide support for community groups, but to train ministers and laymen in new forms of ministry. Subsequent grants in small amounts from the CCMS were to offer some support for the full-time leadership of WSO and its other expenses, but not before WSO had undergone several lean months when no one but the white consultants were drawing salaries. Ironically, the failure of the church forces to stand with WSO against Centennial and the end of direct funding from UTC coincided fairly closely, making the visible signs of interest and commitment on the part of the churches to WSO very faint indeed. Through the first months of 1965 the cadremen knew without doubt that they were free from any threat of manipulation or control from the outside.

CHAPTER IV

THE WELFARE UNION: NEW ROLES

A Welfare Task Force in WSO

The West Side Organization's most successful and sustained activity on behalf of the poor was its welfare union project. It was successful in large part because it fulfilled very important human needs. For the mothers and children who were ensnared in a huge, impersonal, and often ineffective welfare system, WSO provided quick relief in emergencies of many kinds, plus some assurance that there were people--reliable black men--to whom they could turn in any dire circumstance connected with their perilous life on welfare. For the young men of WSO, the welfare action accorded them the deep, masculine satisfaction of being able to act publicly and effectively, within limited range, on behalf of black women and children--to stand up before the "system" and obtain from it the concessions demanded.

The documentary material on the development of the welfare union--Keating's log and my own field notes and reconstruction-- indicate that the cadremen were drawn into direct action as a result of numerous crises in which importunate mothers came to consultants and WSO loyalists for assistance. It was not, as in the case of Centennial Laundry, the choice of WSO leadership to attack the welfare bureaucracy as a symbolic target. The WSO task force on welfare was created in January of 1965, and in a few months became the welfare union, the first such organization of welfare poor in Chicago, and among the very earliest manifestations of what has become the welfare rights movement in the United States. WSO emerged as a possible alternative to total dependency upon the public welfare system and was seized upon by hosts of desperate persons from all over the city of Chicago.

WSO was by no means prepared for such a role--in staff, volunteer resources, finances, or expectations. It happened that it was the white consultants at WSO who responded first in several welfare crises that were laid at the doorstep of WSO. The campaign of action against Centennial was heating up in the fall of 1964 and absorbing the attention of the cadremen. Keating and Strom attempted to deal personally and unobtrusively with a few of the welfare problems brought in, but soon realized that they were touching a situation in which they might easily be inundated with requests to serve as advocates for persons seeking redress of grievances from the welfare system.

Keating's experience began with a woman whose husband was an alcoholic and did not provide for her and her children, one of whom was a fifteen-year-old daughter who was already pregnant and seriously ill. The mother sought relief from a situation in which her

case worker was attempting to force her to work to support the
family and also to have dealings with the father of the daughter's
expected baby, although neither the mother nor the daughter wished
to have any further contact with this man. Keating contacted the
case worker and was told, "Tell these kinds of people that you don't
have time to listen to their story." This incident led the staff to
consider the case worker's attitudes toward the person whom she was
supposedly helping. Robinson summed up his attitude by saying of
the case workers, in general, "They don't know; they've never been
hungry. We know, and we are going to help ourselves."
    The staff agreed to make a representation to Mr. Raymond
Hilliard, Director of the Cook County Department of Public Aid. A
letter was drafted and signed by the staff which was intended to
portray the situation as felt by a welfare suppliant, rather than
by a neutral person. Hilliard was angered by the tone of the representation; the hoped-for outcome, a meeting between upper echelon
Department people and WSO staff, never came off.
    By this time both John Crawford and William Darden had come
into the activists' circle of WSO, having asked for assistance in
dealing with agencies supposedly created to help them with their
employment problems. Crawford's case was emblematic. Unemployed,
he and his family had been receiving welfare while Crawford undertook training in the Manpower Development Training Program, but he
had been unable to obtain employment on the basis of his training.
Meanwhile, his wife was expecting a child, and the Department would
not give them assistance to prepare for its coming. WSO had intervened, through some welfare contacts, to obtain a layette and other
needs for Crawford. He stayed on as a volunteer with WSO, occasionally receiving personal financial assistance from staff members,
and finally becoming a member of the core staff.

Alliances inside the System

    In pursuing the case of Crawford, WSO encountered one district
welfare supervisor who proved to be very valuable to WSO in the
months ahead. She agreed with the cadremen that some of the welfare
administrators could not perceive the real dilemmas of the people.
She became a good interpreter of welfare administration problems to
WSO, coming often to its community meetings and unfailingly responding to requests that she intervene in some critical situation
that WSO had encountered with a welfare family. Also, she helped
the cadremen understand difficult organizational conditions under
which conscientious case workers and supervisors were attempting to
do their jobs; often they were caught by the system, as were the
clients, unable to act responsibly even when they did perceive the
real problems of the people.

The Formation of a Welfare Union

    The organization began asking persons with grievances against
the welfare department to come to the community meetings and tell
their stories. As the cases were presented, the assembled members
were asked what action ought to be taken by WSO to help the complainant. Sometimes a response was agreed upon in the meeting itself,

and volunteers would be assigned to carry it out on the following day. Eventually the community meetings became opportunities for people who had received from WSO the help they required, to "witness" before the community. These meetings were absorbing occasions for people to share their troubles and their victories. The fellowship within WSO was undoubtedly strengthened by them.

The turning point within WSO toward intensive concentration on welfare unionism came in the midst of a crisis within the staff itself. With the court injunction, WSO's direct action campaign against Centennial was brought to a halt in November of 1964. The organization suffered at about the same time the blow of losing its original funding. The few cadremen who had been on salary were off again. The morale was so low that the organization was in danger of losing its initiative within the community. Characteristically, Bob Strom took matters into his own hands by leading a group of WSO loyalists (including, at this time, only one staff member) and a complainant into a welfare district office to make a representation *en masse*. This was clearly a demonstration to make a point because the hour and moment of the sit-in coincided with a deadline at which the complainant was to fulfill a case worker's demand to accept employment as a nurses' aid, even though she had eight children of her own to care for. The protest was against the inhumanity of a threat to force compliance to such a directive by causing not only the client to suffer, but also her children.

This action challenged the staff to begin acting publicly in response to welfare injustices. Not without hesitation, the task was accepted, and specific organizational structures were created to handle welfare activism. Within two weeks more than thirty cases had been represented by WSO people at various district offices, with the threat of another sit-in as the initial bargaining weapon.

In a few months'time, in most cases that threat was no longer necessary to gain redress of grievances. WSO obtained from the Department of Public Aid an interpretation of a ruling which allowed a client to bring a third person into any interview where a complaint or adjustment was being handled. This meant that a complainant could ask for a welfare union representative to accompany her upon any matter of business she might have with the Department, except for the intake interview, which was still reserved for consultation between the client and the case worker. WSO obtained this important concession when, in the first week of May 1965, a group from WSO encountered a rebuff from a hostile district supervisor as it attempted to speak to her for a complainant. The group then threatened to sit-in. The police were called and a compromise was arranged before arrests were necessary. The compromise included the promise of an interview on the following day with an executive from the office of Director Hilliard, in which the policy regarding persons helping complainants deal with case workers and supervisors was to be interpreted.

Hilliard's representative provided some genuine surprises. The supervisor who had provoked the conflict tried to structure the meeting by calling in Strom alone to meet with Hilliard's aid. Strom went in and countered each of the supervisor's interpretations of the problem with illustrations from WSO's file of cases which indicated how recipients felt. The man became interested and asked the WSO representatives to come into the office with Strom in order to speak for themselves. The unhappy supervisor was then required to listen

and note down everything that was said about the case workers, supervisors, and the welfare operation in general. The Department executive then pointed out that Departmental policies allowed for
third persons of the complainant's choice to be present in any
grievance procedure; thus WSO received its organizing technique.
     By the summer of 1965, WSO was heavily engaged in advocacy on
behalf of recipients. WSO announced its intention to organize every
welfare recipient in the city, and to gain from the Department of
Public Aid the recognition of the union as the representative agent
of its clients. Throughout the summer literally hundreds of cases
were handled through the WSO office, and each of the assisted
persons was numbered as a "member" of the union. Members were not
asked to pay dues but show their loyalty to the union by coming to
the community meetings, by helping fellow recipients find their way
to WSO, and by being ready to join an "action" whenever the call
came out.
     Thereafter, the purpose of the community meetings, in addition
to hearing the tales of distress from people on welfare, became that
of training union members in some of the important aspects of welfare law and procedure. In this task WSO received some crucial
assistance from The Reverend William Robinson, a former case worker
with the Department of Public Aid and a staff member of the Chicago
Federation of Christian Churches assigned to welfare problems.
William Robinson often came to WSO on Wednesday nights, and on
Saturday mornings as well, to teach the people about welfare law
and the rights they could legitimately claim under the system. He
spoke particularly to the recipients' fear of the case workers, the
petty politicians, the housing authorities, and others who threatened
loss of aid. He told them that none of those threats were based on
law, that a case worker could not remove anyone from the aid roles
without demonstrating sufficient cause and allowing the recipient
to challenge the evidence with an advocate present. About the
political threats, Robinson could only point toward the time when
the people would have sufficient political power to counteract such
bullying techniques, which were, of course, strictly illegal.

Public Exposure

     WSO now began receiving public notice as an advocate of the
welfare poor in the news media. In December 1965, a committee of
the Illinois State Legislature which considered appropriations for
public aid had scheduled hearings in Springfield and Chicago. WSO
was conspicuously present in both places, having taken bus loads of
citizens hoping to importune the legislature. At these hearings a
sub-committee of the legislators agreed to attend a grievance meeting
at WSO headquarters, an event which was widely covered by the news
media of the city. WSO members told the legislators of their
tenuous and often despairing existence on public aid. For example,
one lady said she had come home after being a patient in the hospital
and found her belongings on the sidewalk. Official welfare policy
is to pay rent only for a limited time while a recipient is in the
hospital; thereafter, no arrangement is made for that person's rent
or belongings if other housing has not been acquired. The recipients
also spoke out about the "detective tactics" of the welfare office--
the policy of coming into the homes of recipients at odd hours hoping

to catch a man in the house. Mrs. B. told of such a person who
visited her house and insisted on searching the premises. Mrs. B.
refused and the investigator threatened to cut off her check.
Chester Robinson's comment on this complaint was published: "This
was just another instance of the difference between constitutional
law and poor peoples' law. What is called illegal search by the
first is okay by the latter."

WBBM-TV, the local CBS affiliate, noted this occasion in a
televised editorial on its evening news program January 11, 1966.
The editorialist took notes of the complaints of the people at the
meeting, checked some of them out, and purportedly found that they
had been "false tear-stories." A woman who complained that her
daughter couldn't go to school because she had no clothing was
found to have a daughter a few days too young to be admitted to
school. Hence, according to WBBM-TV, there was no need to complain
of lack of clothing. The editorial continued:

> Another witness, who described himself as a "worn out, old mule, put
> out to pasture without any grass" complained his relief check had
> been stopped, for some reason. He failed to mention that he had con-
> cealed from the Aid Department an insurance benefit of more than
> $1,000 ten months earlier, and other income he received while drawing
> welfare payments--payments, incidentally, which he has refused to
> pay back although he accepted them fraudulently. Another tale of
> woe came from a man who said the Aid Department gave him unsuitable
> jobs. He didn't mention that it was the Aid Department which trained
> him in the first place, and that he lost each job they arranged for
> him because of drunkenness. . . .For a reason that we don't under-
> stand these people wanted to bite--and bite deeply--the same hand
> that feeds them. . . . Most public aid recipients are grateful for
> assistance, however meager it is, and they try to make the best of
> it. But the display of deceit and plain ingratitude that flooded
> over the advisory hearing, in our view, does a deep injustice to you,
> who contribute to public aid, and those who honestly are in need of
> it.

WSO responded to this attack by publishing the text of WBBM-
TV's editorial and inviting readers to comment. Chester Robinson
asked for, and was given time on February 8 to rebut the editorial
on WBBM-TV. He took pains to show that the station's investigators
had failed to include other qualifying factors in the "false tear-
stories." WSO claimed that the girl was eligible for kindergarten
but had been unable to attend for the reason given. The man for
whom the welfare did not find suitable employment had been trained
as a cook and then hired as a dishwasher and cleaner of rest rooms
at $1.00 per hour. In discouragement he had begun drinking and had
lost his job. WSO then found him a cook's job for which he was
qualified, and he was able to hold it. As for the "worn out mule,"
it was pointed out that this man, Mr. H., was an aged gentlemen of
considerable spirit who had spent all of his working life as a
cotton farmer, a share cropper, in Mississippi. He carried with
him, since coming to Chicago, a small handful of cotton to remind
himself and others of the fruit of his life's labor in the South.
He claimed to have been cheated out of his last crop of cotton by
white men who controlled the cotton gin and who had switched identifying labels on the bales of cotton he had brought to the gin mill.

He believed that he had earned every cent ever given him by welfare.
Should he be asked to give up a small general assistance check and
use the $1,000 he had received from an insurance claim to live from
day to day? Was that a good use of the public's money, or a reward
for a life of hard work?

These cases reveal the real conflicts that arise between the
administration of welfare policy designed to provide a bare subsistence living on a temporary basis, and the human needs of persons
who depend upon welfare for their only stable income. The welfare
union argued that it did not advocate a life on welfare for any
person who can avoid it. But there was no reason why welfare recipients, many of them at least, should accept with shame or with
gratitude the less-than-subsistence income welfare provides. The
WBBM-TV editorial presumed that "reliefers" are unfortunate suppli-
cants upon the body politic. WSO taught that welfare recipients,
on the contrary, belonged to the group of those for whom, as black
persons, slavery had never ended. The welfare support was only a
token of what they, or their ancestors, had worked for all of their
lives. It was the patrimony, meager and unsatisfactory, of their
fathers' centuries-long indenture to the white man.

The leadership of the welfare union received further credence
from the deference of the Chicago Freedom Movement to WSO as the
"best authority" within the Chicago movement upon the problems of
the black welfare poor. Martin Luther King Jr. and his associates,
Andrew Young and James Bevel, spoke in public meetings at WSO and
urged the staff members to bring their experience with welfare
unionism into the Chicago Coordinating Council of Community Organizations, the umbrella group for the King movement which was, in
1965 and 1966, planning its first great urban campaign in the North
for the summer of 1966.

On February 11, 1966, WSO was involved in an action on behalf
of a Mrs. Fannie Staples and her ten children, which resulted eventually in prison sentences of ten days each for Strom, Darden,
Eugene Harris, and Douglas Bryant. The following day, February 12,
WSO had already scheduled a workshop on welfare rights at the organization's headquarters. Quite naturally, the events of the previous
day, when eighteen members of the WSO delegation had been arrested
in the welfare office, were the topic of conversation. After the
usual opening with freedom songs and an inspirational talk by John
Crawford, Bob Strom described the episode. In January Mrs. Staples
had not received her two welfare checks which were the sole financial
support of her family. The reason was that the Department was re-
classifying her case from the category of Aid to Dependent Children-U
(meaning a father was living with the family) to that of General
Assistance. The delay was entirely bureaucratic, but the effect,
in the dead of winter, was that Mrs. Staples was without food for
her children or coal for the stove. WSO had first interceded for
her by phoning the welfare office to ask for emergency assistance.
They were told it would be forthcoming and that, meanwhile, they
should obtain food from a neighborhood store which the Department
would instruct to provide for her needs. The store refused to comply
without an official disbursement order from the Department. WSO
went to the Aid Office for the order and was told it was impossible
to obtain before the next day. Another trip was made to the merchant
who again refused groceries on credit alone. The party went back
again to the welfare office and decided to sit-in until a disbursement order was written that afternoon to care for the needs of the

family. The police were called, and the entire group was put under
arrest. Bail bond was obtained, and the group was all present at
the workshop meeting to recount the story.

Mrs. Staples was introduced after Strom, and she retold the
entire story herself. She was a young woman, in her early thirties,
and she spoke emotionally, yet very simply and movingly. Her husband
had been unable to hold a job, and, for some reason, her case worker
insisted that she be shifted from ADC-U to General Assistance, a
distinction she did not understand. The supervisor had encouraged
her to get temporary help from her friends and her sisters while
the arrangements were worked out between Chicago and Springfield.
But these other persons were also living on welfare and had no resources to help her.

William Robinson next picked up the story and used it to
illustrate his lecture on the rights and procedures open to welfare
clients in such situations. The shift from ADC-U to General Assistance was usually made, he said, to put control of difficult cases
in the hands of the State of Illinois, so they could be handled
without having to comply with federal guidelines for ADC. This was
desirable from the point of view of the local welfare professionals,
though hardly so from that of the recipient. The state category
allows for food disbursements and other controls on the client's
spending, which cannot be had under ADC. Apparently the welfare
worker believed that Mrs. Staples had been unable to control her
husband's spending of the welfare check and that the use of disbursements would insure that the money went for the essentials.
There had been no chance for the recipient to argue her own position,
nor had there been a provision to care for the family while the ad-
justments were being made. Under no circumstances were the children
considered responsible for the behavior of the father, nor was the
wife to be held accountable for her husband; yet the system worked
its hardships chiefly upon them. (Mrs. Staples had been promised
an emergency coal requisition on Monday of the following week *if* she
appeared at the welfare office *with* her husband.)

William Robinson then spoke of the strength in many black
families where the mother alone is present and is the head of the
family, countering sociological interpretations to the contrary,
and pointing out that he himself was the product of such a family.
Yet welfare policy reflected the assumption that a father *ought* to
be present with every family whatever the cost in other hardships
they might endure.

The case itself became a celebrated instance of WSO's advocacy
of the welfare poor and its method of using resources inside the
community, and outside as well, in representing those who were caused
to suffer. The fact that several of the actors served jail sentences
thereafter for having stood with Mrs. Staples and her children was
well remembered whenever WSO's welfare program was explained.

A Case Study of Welfare Advocacy

The material which follows is a description of an action which
occurred about six months later, in which I was a participant. By
this time WSO was at the height of its activities as a welfare union,
operating four offices in various parts of the city through which
welfare complaints were pursued. This action is described in full
because it is a good example of how WSO moved when it felt required

to do so, and why it was successful in obtaining from the welfare
system the immediate assistance required.

In August of 1966 WSO had established contact with the Englewood Civic Organization which had been trying, rather unsuccessfully,
to help several of its constituent families with welfare problems.
On August 21 their leaders came to WSO headquarters with a problem
they had not been able to handle and sought the aid of the more experienced welfare unionists.

Two women who were living on ADC with no little courage and
initiative, had set out to fight the landlord who owned the decrepit
building in Englewood in which they, and seven other tenant families,
had been living. On their own, the women organized a rent strike
beginning in May of 1966. They had been unsuccessful in gaining
the full support of the other tenants because, they believed, their
case worker had influenced the other welfare clients in the building
not to cooperate. Since May, the women had withheld their rent
money, which was part of their welfare allowance from the Department
of Public Aid, trying to force the landlord to make essential re-
pairs. Meanwhile, the Englewood Civic Organization worker had
attempted to construct a legal case for the rent strike by summoning
building inspectors from the Department of Public Aid, by taking
pictures of literally dozens of code violations in their apartments,
and by bringing the case into court for a hearing. The Department
had sent a building inspector to testify at the hearing, but he had
refused to testify that the landlord was in violation of the codes.
The photographs were not admitted as evidence, though they obviously
contradicted the building inspector's testimony, and the judge refused to allow the complaint.

The frustration of the two women was exacerbated by the fact
that their case worker had acceded to the landlord's request to have
the rental portion of their monthly checks, beginning in August,
disbursed directly to him; thus the women could no longer exercise
control over the payment of rent.

In early summer of 1966 the Department of Public Aid had issued
a directive controlling much more stringently the use of disbursement orders with welfare clients whom the case worker believed were
unable to manage their own finances. In other words, in this directive the recipient *gained* a larger measure of independence *vis-a-vis*
the case worker because the latter could no longer direct a disbursement order to be given, instead of cash, without showing a strong
case for the inability of the client to manage his or her own money.
Therefore, in the matter of rental disbursements for the two women
who had withheld rent for three months, the welfare union believed
it had a very strong grievance against the case worker who had
effectively cut off their power to force a landlord to maintain
their building. The women had not spent the rent money, for which
they could have been punished by losing their welfare support entirely, but had held it, and were ready to produce it when the landlord fulfilled *his* obligations. The case worker had caused the
August rent to be paid anyway, and their meager access to power had
been removed.

Further, the women charged the case worker with turning the
other client residents in the building against them by ordering all
rents in the building paid with disbursement orders, and even
threatening to cut away their other welfare support if they went
along on the rent strike. The case worker had violated

their confidence as clients by divulging information about them to other clients in the block, a severe charge indeed against the professional practice of welfare service. Finally, they themselves had not received their welfare checks for food and other necessities that week and were told that the money was being withheld by action of the case worker.

With these charges, WSO felt it was ready to do battle for the oppressed recipients and, at the same time, show the Englewood Civic Organization how welfare unionism is conducted. The action began with a group from WSO, led by myself, and made up of the three ECO representatives, the two women making the complaint, one friend who had come to give support, and another white man who had come to observe. We proceeded to the Englewood District Office, where we were to meet the WSO regulars--Bill Darden, John Crawford, Curtis Beard, and Bob Strom--who were coming from another appointment. However, the second group did not arrive as expected, so I began the task of stating our business to the receptionist and asking to see the case worker. It was evident that our arrival caused some consternation in the office. Although it was 11:30 a.m., we were quickly told that the particular case worker, Mr. D., had gone out to lunch. We were to wait in the reception room for his return.

At Englewood the reception room is similar to that in most district offices--rows of hard wooden benches lined up in church pew fashion, facing a reception desk near the front. In these offices recipients must wait, sometimes for hours, to contract their business with the case workers and supervisors. When summoned to the interview they go to a large room of semi-private cubicles, which have no doors. There are no magazines or newspapers in the waiting room, no toys to entertain children, nor any of the other amenities of a pleasant public facility. I noted that the men's toilet contained no wash basin.

At 12:35 p.m. Bob Strom arrived with the WSO leaders. I reported to them that we had waited an hour for the case worker to return, and they scoffed at my evident lack of aggressiveness in the setting. Without hesitation, Darden went to the receptionist and asked to see the supervisor of the case worker. He was on vacation, but a replacement was located, a Mrs. B., and we all were led at once back to the interview room to meet her in one of the cubicles. The absurdity of twelve of us trying to crowd into a six-by-six cubicle was soon evident, and the meeting was moved upstairs to the conference room, a large room with a long wooden table, comfortable chairs, wall charts, etc.

The supervisor began the session by announcing that Mr. D. was still out to lunch, and we would begin without him. She asked that one of us state the grievances, and Darden insisted that the women speak for themselves. They told their story well, reflecting a strong feeling that Mr. D. treated them in a very degrading manner, "as if we were less than human." At that point Mr. D. entered the room. He proved to be a young black man, very smartly groomed, and apparently very tense. The women went on to tell of the problems in their building, charging that Mr. D. had actually made the neighbors antagonistic toward them by threatening to withhold checks. They testified that another building inspector from Public Aid had come to inspect and had agreed with them that the building was below standard. He had promised to recommend that the building be put on a list of residences for which the Department of Public Aid would itself refuse to pay rent until it had been rehabilitated. (This was another inspector than the one who had refused to testify at the court hearing.) But even after this, Mr. D. had issued a disbursement order covering the rent, and had withheld their support checks which had been due the weekend before August 11.

Mr. D. was asked to respond to these charges. He did so by saying that these people were not telling the whole truth, and they knew it. Strom pressed him to answer a specific question. Did he or did he not discuss the private information he received as a case worker with the other people in the building? Strom's manner was very forceful. Mrs. B. broke in to say that she was going to conduct a quiet meeting, with no antagonism. Strom said, "I *am* antagonistic to Mr. D., and I want that understood from the beginning." Mr. D. bristled and replied, "Oh you are!" The supervisor insisted again on calm and quiet, and Darden, sitting on her left, joked a little, which relieved some of the pressure.

The supervisor then announced that the charges against Mr. D. would be discussed with him privately--that he did not have to defend himself or his actions in this company. She promised further to take up the matter of listing the building as sub-standard with the authorities downtown, particularly Mr. Spillone, whose responsibility was housing for welfare recipients. She had hoped that this statement would conclude the meeting, but Darden startled her by reporting that WSO had come just that morning from a meeting with Mr. Spillone, and knew exactly how to proceed in matters like this one.

Strom asked permission to question further. The case worker agreed to discuss the situation with them, although he needn't do so, saying, "These two ladies know why they are here today." The supervisor interjected to point out that discussing the cases meant revealing confidences to unauthorized persons, namely the WSO and ECO representatives, and this she couldn't permit. Strom pointed out that there had been a ruling over a year ago allowing recipients to bring other parties with them into a consultation regarding a grievance, and that the women had done this in asking WSO to represent them. Mrs. B. then consented but insisted that the women sign a statement giving permission for their case to be reviewed in this company. They agreed, and Mrs. B. left to dictate a statement of permission.

The discussion then moved to the propriety of Mr. D.'s action in sending a disbursing order for rent money to the landlord. Mr. D. replied that he had no authority to give the women permission to withhold rent money. Darden then pressed him by asking whether it was not his *duty* to act primarily *in* the interest of the clients, and if so, why had he acted *against* the interest of the clients, and in *support* of the interests of the landlord? The women knew the legal risk involved in not paying rent, but he, their advocate in the welfare service, actually refused to let them act on their own behalf, much less to help them.

Strom then demanded to know why he had ordered the rent money changed to a disbursement order. Mr. D. replied simply that the landlord had asked him to do it. He was asked whether he knew the building had been inspected recently by a welfare housing authority. He replied that he knew it had, but admitted that he had not checked to see what the inspector's report had been before authorizing the disbursal order to be sent to the landlord. He was asked about the

withholding of support checks for the two clients, and answered
that it had now been taken care of, but he gave no explanation of
why he had held up the checks in the first place. WSO pointed out
sharply that the case worker had no legal right, under the welfare
code, to withhold checks arbitrarily, or even to threaten to do so.
     The supervisor then left to call Spillone, and Mr. D. got up
to leave. Darden said, "Just wait a few minutes, Mr. D. I thought
Mr. D. was going to stay in here [when Mrs. B. left] so we could
have some fun." Mr. D. snapped back, "I don't regard this as a
game." Strom retorted grimly, "Neither do we, Mr. D."
     The supervisor returned with the word that Spillone's office
was busy, but she agreed to act at once to block the further use
of disbursement orders for rent in the building. She also promised
to send letters to all of the clients in the building, ordering
them to ignore the notices they had received from the Department of
Public Aid which informed them that rent funds were being disbursed
directly to the landlord. This notice was now cancelled. We asked
about the money for the woman who had not been given her support
check for over a week. The supervisor agreed to type out a check
order at once, which we would then bear to the treasurer's office
at Damen and Madison, where emergency checks were issued.
     While waiting for the check order in the Englewood Office,
Darden, Crawford,and Strom were active in the reception room. They
found one person who had been waiting all day to see a supervisor,
and they demanded that she be shown in at once. It was done. They
then discovered a sick woman who had wanted to go to a hospital and
had come to the District Office to get a statement saying she should
be admitted for treatment. She, too, had waited all day for a
supervisor. Again the men demanded she be given immediate attention,
and it was done. Mr. D. appeared with the letters and orders in
hand. He and Darden shook hands and held a strained but moderately
friendly conversation before the group left.
     The atmosphere of this meeting was alternately tense and light.
WSO obviously had the goods on Mr. D., and Mrs. B. had all she
could do to protect him (which was her responsibility) until she
could deal with the case in a professional way. Strom and Darden
carried the ball in the meeting, and I was told later it was typical
for the two of them to agree beforehand who was to be tough, hostile,
and demanding, and who was to give the light touch. Darden had done
the latter, and was able to leave both Mrs. B. and Mr. D. smiling,
though shaken. The result was satisfactory from WSO's standpoint.
The women had their checks, the dispersal orders were to be cancelled,
and the Englewood Office had felt the direct power of WSO. Moreover,
the women had been given a chance to speak their grievances in a
situation where they were not the underdogs, but had meaningful
support. The case worker was humiliated and, even though protected
from the charges, he had been forced to admit that he had, at the
very least, not acted on behalf of his clients.

The Need for Advocacy

     In the summer of 1966 a law student from Northwestern University,
Richard A. Devine, made a study of all the files which WSO had com-
piled for the purpose of ascertaining (1) whether there were indeed
grievances against the Cook County Department of Public Aid which

represented the denials of basic rights to welfare clients under
the law, and what if anything was being done to resolve them, and
(2) whether the recipient needs some form of representation to insure that his rights to due process are adequately protected, and
if so, what type of organization is best equipped to do this.
    Devine found on file in WSO 275 cases which had been handled
in the first year, from which he drew a sample of 75. At this time
WSO was claiming to have handled successfully more than 1,000 complaints. This is not an unreasonable assumption considering that
portfolios of files in other "local" offices were not available to
Devine and that WSO did not keep strict account of these records.
    Devine's report notes that, according to the Biennial
Report of the Commission on Public Aid and Assistance, out of
132,305 informal and formal application denials in the state of
Illinois from July 1963 to June 1964, there were a total of 105
appeals. These were appeals on denials of applications to receive
welfare. WSO had not yet found an adequate means of representing
a complainant in this area, for third parties were not admitted to
"intake" interviews at the time applications were reviewed. However,
the tremendous disparity between denials and appeals in this aspect
of welfare work indicates the inaccessibility of the welfare system
to appeals from the clients themselves. WSO was clearly involved
in an area of real need--representing the welfare client.
    Devine's research noted five major categories in which the
grievances were listed:

    1. Declared ineligible because [client] failed to meet one of
        the following requirements: residence; insufficient rec-
        ords to establish age, lack of support, whereabouts of
        husband; failure of the husband to come into the Public
        Aid Office; sufficient income to support the family.
    2. Delay in processing the application.
    3. Grant reduced without adequate explanation.
    4. Grant cancelled or held up because of failure to accept
        employment when client was deemed "employable."
    5. Assistance inadequate for the needs of the family.

    Of 80 complainants in the Devine sample, 69 were women. The
number of children per complainant was 4.83, with the largest in
any one family being 14. Information on age was available for 59
of the complainants, and of these, 21 were in their twenties, 23 in
their thirties, 11 in their forties, 2 in their fifties, and 2 in
their sixties. 44 of the 59 were between twenty and thirty-nine
years of age.
    Devine coded expressions found in the files indicating the
clients' attitudes to case workers, and he rated these attitudes
on a scale of 1-5. Of 44 complainants, 3 indicated they considered
their case worker to be "very good" or "very nice" or "most helpful."
12 expressed some sort of favorable feeling for the case worker.
8 give contradictory or inconsistent statements about the case
worker. 9 expressed a mild or moderate dislike, and 12 expressed
a distinct dislike for the case worker. 15 people, therefore,
expressed some sort of favorable attitude toward their case worker,
while 21 had unfavorable attitudes.

WSO, An Ally of Public Aid

In May of 1966 WSO joined the Independent Union of Public Aid Employees in a strike to gain bargaining power for the union with the Department of Public Aid. WSO manned picket lines and announced support for the case workers in the union who were striking, in part, to foster reforms within the system. The *Torch* published the strikers'"Manifesto" on May 19, 1966, which declared the existing welfare system to be "inhumane," and outlined reforms which the union would attempt to instigate through its bargaining power.

As a result of the strike, the union won its right to a bargaining position with the Department, and WSO felt that it had established strong alliances within the Department itself among case workers with whom it had manned picket lines. The following summer, whenever a grievance was to be processed in a welfare office, WSO looked for, and received, support from friendly officials, including a few supervisors who had joined the Independent Union. Two case workers spent their days off working directly with WSO in its welfare organizing.

Less than a year later the situation changed due to the appointment of WSO's enthusiastic supporter, William Robinson, as Public Aid Director. In May of 1967, the new Director found his administration faced with another strike by the Independent Union. This was a "bread and butter" strike for higher case work salaries and other benefits. WSO was faced with a difficult issue and dealt with it by asking the case workers' union to agree to honor WSO strike demands for more benefits to recipients in the future--that is, to refuse to cross WSO picket lines if and when WSO acted for changes within the welfare system. The president of the case workers' union, the Reverend Douglas Cater, indicated that WSO was making impossible demands, and that the case workers would never agree to honor a recipients' picket line. WSO then sided instead with its ally, Robinson, by providing recipients to man the welfare offices during the strike, in order to keep the flow of aid moving to the poor. This proved to be an important personal experience for several recipients, who received a sense of dignity in helping others, plus satisfaction in performing tasks which they had been considered too unskilled or unreliable to perform.

WSO followed this experience with a proposal to the Department of Public Aid to help the Department train capable recipients in welfare work, interpreting welfare provisions to other recipients, and relaying to case workers and supervisors the real needs of persons to whom professional case workers had been unable to relate effectively. The Department responded with a memorandum marked "for discussion only." On the basis of this memo, constructive conversations were conducted by the Department with WSO and other groups representing welfare recipients. The memo stated clearly that it was not legally authorized "to recognize or enter into a contract with any group of welfare applicants or recipients." However, it interpreted its responsibilities to include working "in a *constructive* relationship with interested parties and community organizations, including welfare unions."

The memo stated clearly the policy of recipient representation in grievance matters under which WSO had been conducting its welfare union activities for the past two years. It declared that "Membership or participation in any group, organization, or welfare union

in no way jeopardizes an eligible individual's right to assistance."
The memo concluded with four "Recommendations Under Consideration."

A. The Department will consider and support desirable standards
    of assistance such as have been recommended by one welfare
    union. The recommendation for increased allowances for
    school lunches, and for carfare for school attendance, as
    has been proposed, is endorsed by this Department.

B. In response to recommendations received from individuals
    and groups, the Agency plans to reorganize and move the
    Welfare Rehabilitation Service to a new and improved
    location, to provide better services to applicants and
    recipients.

C. At the request of several individuals, the Department is
    planning a proposal to secure federal funds for the employ-
    ment of recipients as district office community representa-
    tives and family agency coordinators. The Department will
    ask the help of the organizations and unions in recruiting
    such employees.

D. The Department recommends that Advisory Boards or Commit-
    tees to district offices be formed. One such board, com-
    prised of former and current representatives of local groups
    organized in the community, is in existence in the area
    served by the Garfield Office.

Conclusion

It would be difficult to prove that any of these innovations in
welfare administration and case work are the direct result of WSO
welfare union activity. But it is a fact that WSO welfare union
activity prepared a group of people for participation in the type of
community relations program the Department's memo envisioned, and
laid some groundwork for the public's acceptance of recipients'
participation in the administration of Public Aid. Certainly there
were real gains for the dependent poor in their struggle to achieve
representation in the councils of decision which affect their fate.

CHAPTER V

IN DEFENSE OF THE COMMUNITY

Friendly Intervention

Tuesday, July 12, 1966, was the next to last day of a long, intense heat wave that kept Chicagoans sweltering in 90° heat for more than a week. The eastern edge of the huge, West Side ghetto begins about three miles from Lake Michigan, separated from its prevailing breezes and public beaches by the concrete canyons of the Loop area, several railroad yards, the Dan Ryan Expressway, and industrial properties. Throughout the hot spell, long lines of children waited to enter the few park district swimming pools available within the ghetto. The hours for swimming were strictly regulated according to age groups and, in some cases, according to the neighborhoods from which the swimmers came. For the ghetto youngsters the most immediate source of relief from the steaming tenements and pavements were the city fire hydrants.

Although it is against the city ordinance to turn hydrants on except in emergencies, generations of Chicago children have frolicked in water gushing into the street from wide-open hydrants. Usually someone will improvise a spray system by propping a board against the open hydrant valve. In this way dozens of youngsters can play at a single hydrant. The police are known to be fairly tolerant about these minor infractions of the law, usually leaving the hydrants on until the danger of the street being flooded, or complaints from third floor apartment residents that the water pressure is too low, prompt a policeman to move in on the scene and turn the water off. Mayor Richard Daley admitted to having played in hydrants during his boyhood in the old Bridgeport Irish neighborhood just south of the present West Side ghetto.

During that excruciatingly long hot spell the hydrants had been turned on and off, again and again, in block after block in the inner city. Motorists driving the side streets were forced to keep their windows rolled up against the spray. Also, one drove with eyes peeled for sleek, brown bodies heedlessly running and tumbling through the water.

In the late afternoon of that Tuesday, Chester Robinson was seated on the sidewalk outside the storefront headquarters on Roosevelt Road. With him, trying to cool off, were several of his staff members and friends from the Near West Side community.

According to Robinson's description of the events that afternoon, at about 6:30 p.m. two police cars driving west on Roosevelt Road suddenly made a sharp U-turn in the middle of the block and pulled up in front of WSO headquarters. A police sergeant asked Robinson whether he had any influence with the teenagers in the community, and he replied that he did. The officer explained that some

49

of the youngsters at the corner of Roosevelt Road and Throop Street
were creating a disturbance. In Robinson's words: "He said that
someone had been robbed and that the young boys were stopping cars,
pulling people out, and throwing them in the water." Robinson
agreed to go with the police to the scene, just two and one-half
blocks east of WSO, to talk with the teenagers.   Until this time
Robinson had not known of any trouble in the area, although he knew
that fire hydrants had been turned on here and there.

When they arrived at the corner, Robinson found that the chief
problem concerned the driver of an ice cream truck whose vehicle
had fallen into a hole. The driver had gone into a store to phone
for a tow truck. While his truck was unattended, some of the
youngsters entered it and helped themselves to a few ice cream bars
and other treats. That trouble appeared to have ended by the time
Robinson arrived. The children were preoccupied splashing one
another from the flood of water in the street. The hydrant itself
had been turned off by the police on the scene. One of the police
cars left the corner, evidently expecting no further trouble.

The youngsters were intent on keeping the hydrant open and
soon had it flowing again, in spite of the police presence. Shortly,
two more squad cars came to the corner, and a dispute arose about
letting the water stay on. One argument used by the youngsters was
that the hydrants were being allowed to run over on Taylor Street,
the main east-west artery in a small Italian neighborhood just two
blocks north of Roosevelt Road. Robinson urged the officers not
to insist that the hydrant be shut off just yet, because it would
only make the youngsters more defiant. Also, more and more people
were being attracted to the scene by the presence of the police
cars. His warning went unheeded, and the water was turned off.
Again the assisting police cars left.

As Robinson sat in the remaining car talking with the police,
he saw a crowd of people surround the hydrant. They were shielding
from the sight of the patrol car someone who was bent on turning
the hydrant on again. For a few minutes the water flowed freely.
Then the policeman in the squad car gave his partner a wrench and
told him to cut the water off. As the officer was in the process
of turning the valve he was doused by someone in the crowd. According to Robinson, the victim was amused by the incident, but not so
his partner, who had spotted the offender. He went over to the
crowd, grabbed the boy, and led him back to the police car. Suddenly a pulling and shoving match began between the police and the
crowd. The boy was pulled free, and the police were prevented from
chasing him by the crowd.

Interceding in the Midst of Disorder

At that point, for the first time that afternoon, bricks and
bottles were thrown. Two of these missiles hit the windshield of
the police car. Robinson got out of the car and walked across the
street. The officers radioed for help, and shortly thereafter almost thirty police cars were at the scene. The crowd had grown
much larger and angrier, and the police found themselves in a club-
swinging melee, with five or six teenagers taking blows on the head.
Newspapers attest to the fact that blood was spilled as several of
the fighters were subdued and arrested by the police. Several

persons who had come to the street to see what was going on found themselves being shoved and beaten by the police who were attempting to move the crowd off the corner.

To Robinson the affair seemed completely out of hand, with bricks and bottles being thrown at all passing vehicles, whether or not they were police cars. So he returned to WSO on foot, where he immediately phoned the police department and asked to talk with the commander of the district. The commander was on sick leave, so Robinson spoke with a lieutenant who was asked to come over to the scene to control the police. Robinson said he could control the people, he believed, if someone else would stop the aggressive police action. Robinson and others also called others, including Dr. Martin Luther King Jr., Don Benedict of the Chicago City Missionary Society, and Archie Hargraves. James Bevel and James Orange of the Southern Christian Leadership Conference staff had already gotten the word and were at WSO.

Two other WSO staff persons, John Crawford and Gene Harris, had remained in the troubled area and were attempting a tactic of their own to try to cool the disturbance. The riot was now about one hour old and a make-shift line had been established with the people facing the police, shouting and throwing missiles, to which the police responded with forcible attempts to disperse the crowd. A chanting taunt had begun somehow with the people singing in a low voice the phrase from "The Volga Boatman"--dah-dah-da-a-a-a-dah-Ugh! Gene Harris saw in this chant a chance to get the people moving away from the trouble area. He began singing the words "Come on to WSO--Ugh!" He called to John Crawford, the regular freedom song leader in the organization, to get the people singing these words and keep it going. Soon the word had been communicated, and more than a hundred people were on the move up the block toward the storefront headquarters.

Unfortunately, from the point of view of Crawford and Harris, the police saw fit to follow the crowd closely, and before long the mass was gathered outside the storefront with the police in the street and on the other side--the north side--of Roosevelt Road. Chester Robinson believed, by this time, that the secret to stopping the whole thing was to convince the police to withdraw their cars and troops to some point a block away, while they, as local leaders, attempted to deal with the people. Also they felt it would be an ameliorative act on behalf of the police if they would release the young men already taken into custody during the earlier stages of the battle. The men talked in these terms with the police captain on the scene, but their request was denied. Later, in the press accounts, the police contended that they had acceded to just such a request from Puerto Rican community leaders during the early stages of the rioting in Chicago's Division Street neighborhood earlier that summer. It hadn't worked. Therefore, they refused to pull back from the immediate area of conflict in front of WSO.

Crawford's attempts to organize a meeting inside WSO were of little avail because of the continuing confusion outside. Meanwhile, it had rained briefly, which may have helped bring a lull in the violence on the street. But the tension was still very high, and occasional bricks and insults were thrown at the police across the street, provoking, at one point, a movement of police to the door of WSO itself, where another melee occurred. Again several persons were hurt.

Throughout the early evening WSO headquarters became the hub
of furious activity. The press and television people, police
officers, precinct officials, ministers, and community residents
of all ages crowded in and out. The two telephones rang continuously
as newspeople from around the city and country attempted to find out
what was happening. It is important to realize that the teenagers
and young men who had been aroused during the earlier conflict with
the police also came and went freely, thus making WSO a kind of
neutral ground where communication among all parties was going on
at all times. Robinson, Bill Darden, and the other WSO leaders were
consulted by belligerents from the street gangs, as well as by police
officials, youth agency personnel, and others who were trying desperately to cool the riot.

Attempts to Give Leadership

At about 10:00 p.m. a meeting was to be held two blocks west of
WSO headquarters in the Shiloh Baptist Church. Efforts were made to
move the crowds in and around WSO, and especially the young men,
over to the church were Dr. King wanted to talk with them. Robinson
went with King and Andrew Young to the meeting, while John Crawford,
Jim Orange, Bill Darden, Archie Hargraves, and several others from
WSO and SCLC remained on the outside circulating among the hundreds
of people who were unable, or unwilling, to go into the church.
The crowds, inside and outside, were restless, and it was evident
that trouble was building up. Dr. King's efforts to reason with
the group inside the church were ineffectual. Many on the outside
refused to hear King, declaring that they did not want to be talked
to about nonviolence in the face of what they were convinced was
police brutality.
Robinson, who was on the platform with King and Bevel, suggested to these leaders organizing another march, this time leading
the crowd toward the police station on Racine and Monroe, where, he
believed, scores of arrested teenagers were being held. (Dr. King
had secured the release of six young men who were the first to be
arrested.) Robinson had in mind the successful effort of Crawford
and Harris in moving the crowds away from the Throop Street trouble
area earlier that evening, a move which had temporarily cooled the
violence and, indeed, might have ended the entire affair except for
the continued presence of police in front of WSO. This idea was
not accepted by the other civil rights leaders. The session in the
church deteriorated in confusion with speakers unable to hold their
audience. At the last moment, the WSO Director attempted, from the
platform, to organize a march to the district station. He was unsuccessful. This was interpreted in the press as a sign of Robinson's
unwillingness to accept Dr. King's leadership, his inability to lead
the people of his neighborhood, and WSO's excessive militancy.

Physical Intervention

Outside, the crowd of more than a thousand people was becoming
more aroused. Young men collected garbage cans and barrels and set
up a road block on Ashland Avenue near 13th Street. A car carrying
three Puerto Ricans approached the road block from the south and

failed to turn back in time to avoid being entrapped by the crowd. Someone cried, "Let's get 'em!" and suddenly scores of teenagers attacked and began pummeling the car. They threw ash cans onto the car, broke out all of the windows,and pulled the three from the car with the evident intent of beating them. Bill Clark from WSO jumped in front of the men being pulled from the car and confronted the attackers with the command to lay off, or fight him first. The two terrified Puerto Ricans (one had managed to escape on foot) were ordered by Clark to sit down, and Clark was joined immediately by Hargraves and two others who formed a human shield against the mob for the two men on the ground. Hargraves has given Bill Clark credit for perhaps saving the lives of these two men. The police were at that moment several blocks away at the intersection of Roosevelt and Ashland, and in a poor position to come to their defense in time. In Hargraves' words,

> Everybody will remember the real bravery of Bill Clark. If he had not made that break, or if someone else had made that break, not being Bill, I guess they would have been killed, because Bill has that kind of respect for physical power among the teenagers. And they hesitated. They were almost ready to jump on him. But they hesitated when Bill said, "You gotta beat me if you are goin' to beat these guys." This is the thing that ought to get into the record somewhere.

Significantly, the story of this remarkable act of bravery on the part of one man, a WSO leader, did not get into the press accounts, although the incident is well-documented by the testimony of Hargraves and other observers.

With Clark and the others preserving a stand-off with the rioters, the police reached the scene. Clark told the teenagers to scatter if they didn't want to be arrested. The police started toward the small group of adults who were protecting the men on the ground with clubs swinging. Hargraves called to one policeman whom he recognized and told him to lay off, as they were protecting the Puerto Ricans.

At about that instant, other police down the street began shooting in the air; from then on the rioting and rampaging reached its most serious proportions. Dr. King and his staff, with Robinson and the WSO people, returned to WSO feeling that not much could be done at that moment on the streets.

For the rest of that long night until well past 2:00 a.m., WSO remained the focal point for all kinds of activity. King and his people worked from there as did police officers from the Human Relations detachment of the Chicago police. Youth agency street workers were in and out. WSO was used as a communications center by the teenagers and young men, some of whom were no doubt involved in the rioting, but also others who were attempting to make contact with gang leaders in the streets on behalf of Chester Robinson. Dick Gregory was present that evening and made several sorties with Robinson into the streets to talk with rioters. Finally, King and the others left, and WSO staffers settled down to spend the few hours before dawn in relative quiet.

Organizing a Community Response

The following morning, July 13, Dr. King and his staff were again at WSO. Efforts were begun to organize a noon-hour community meeting at the Community Presbyterian Church, another storefront institution directly across the street from WSO. The meeting was to bring together the local businessmen (some of whom already had suffered considerable property damage), the civil rights leaders, the community agency representatives, ministers, and some of the gang leaders who had participated in the events of the night before. Dr. King, Andrew Young, and Chester Robinson chaired the meeting, which was very long. Grievances were aired by the teenagers against the police and the businessmen, in particular.

King and Robinson had announced a press conference at WSO to follow the meeting, but the press and TV people did not wait for the meeting at the church to end before they opened a press conference of their own with the gang members and others who had crowded into WSO in the meantime.

At 2:00 p.m. this rump press conference ended,and some of the crowd dispersed. Excitement was still very high. The afternoon was again very hot, and hydrants were running on Roosevelt Road and in the back streets. WSO and SCLC staff circulated up and down the streets talking with the people.

The police were watchful all afternoon. Whenever a police vehicle passed along the street, people whistled and jeered. The police did not again interfere with the water play in the hydrants, which now had a definitely defiant meaning. At evening, according to Robinson, the police made the same mistake they had made the night before. The hydrants were repeatedly and forcibly turned off. Bricks began to fly. The long-awaited cool front reached the Near West Side of Chicago that evening, but the weather was no longer a factor affecting the behavior of the angry people.

Although Wednesday evening was the regular time of meeting for WSO, John Crawford and others had thought no meeting would go on that night. However, as the trouble intensified in the area and more and more people around the city learned that the "juvenile fracas"--as it had been reported in the morning presses--was actually a serious rebellion in the Near West Side ghetto, crowds of people began flocking to WSO. Eventually, the room was packed from front to rear with young people, mothers and children, adult men from the community, civil rights leaders, ministers, politicians, police representatives, and even several others from outside the community. At last a meeting was called to order, and it was announced that the teen leaders were to be given a chance to speak their grievances in the presence of Police Task Force Commander Hackett. Speaker after speaker made allegations of police brutality and insensitivity related not only to the night before but to countless other incidents prior to the riot. The police representatives met complaint after complaint with responses which did nothing to alleviate the intense hostility. They defended the police action and issued moral instructions on law and order. Eventually, most of the gang leaders stalked out of the meeting and into the street. Later on it was discovered that while the meeting was in progress, some of the gang members were outside in the alley making molotov cocktails.

Much of the huge crowd remained to hear John Crawford and others speak. The attitude in WSO throughout the entire riot

sequence was that police themselves had provoked the violence by
their tactics in quelling a very minor incident of juvenile defi-
ance. Crawford castigated the men of the community for fighting
the police in a cowardly way and with no productive purpose. He
said that the young men had thrown bricks and bottles, but then fled
to safety behind the women and children when the police threatened
to shoot. Crawford did not attempt, as Dr. King had done, to advocate nonviolence as a norm of behavior for this situation. He
came out against the irrational, purposeless actions of the gangs
and the mob. His immediate purpose was to end the rioting that was
threatening to rise to new fury in the streets. But he did not
deny the need to fight in some more purposeful way to end police
brutality.

   At about 10:00 p.m. the atmosphere was very tight inside and
outside of WSO. The headquarters was literally jammed with people,
and the sounds of rioting came in from the street. At one point
it was announced that the people of the neighborhood had "to get
themselves together," and that all the whites in the room had to
leave. This put the white people outside on the sidewalk just as
the molotov cocktails and weapons fire were coming into full play.
The situation proved frightening, but not harmful, and eventually
all the whites left the area safely. Later on, it was agreed generally that the rioting at no time was a manifestation of specific
anti-white feeling, although crowd reactions are unpredictable in
such a situation. The behavior of the most active participants indicated primarily a reaction against police power, with black policemen having just as hard a time of it as white.

   The result of the strategy meeting was that the district police
commander was approached with a suggestion that WSO be allowed to
patrol the riot areas to talk with the people and to ask them to go
inside their homes. Two teams of fifteen men each were set up, with
John Crawford and Archie Hargraves as leaders, to walk the area
west and east of Halsted Avenue. The police agreed to give the
patrols access to all side streets and alleys upon the use of the
password, "Peace." The teams went out around 11:00 p.m. and worked
the area until 1:30 or 2:00 a.m., by which time the fighting and
shooting were stopped. According to Hargraves, with the exception
of sporadic looting throughout that night, that was the end of the
rioting on the Near West Side for the rest of the summer. The next
night's action was several miles farther west in the Lawndale and
Garfield Park ghetto areas. It was there that the National Guard
was eventually called to restore order.

Nerve Center

   Although the rioting was over on the Near West Side, WSO remained the center of feverish activity throughout the next days.
By Wednesday afternoon the national press, radio, and TV people had
come to regard WSO as a prime news center for all that was happening
in Chicago's troubled West Side. The Wednesday press conference
was only the beginning. Reporters came in droves requesting interviews with Chester Robinson, if possible, or with almost anyone
else who would talk with them. The news coverage of WSO's involve-
ment in these events is a study in itself. In general, the impres-
sion of the role WSO was playing was left largely ambiguous. Witness

the failure to report the actions of Clark, Hargraves,and the others
in the street on Tuesday night. On July 20 Chicago's *American* published an interview by a *New York Post* reporter with Chester Robinson.
In the story, Robinson was described as "an ex-dope pusher" who was
the "street-smart boss" of the "militant" West Side Organization and
who was involved, in some vague and unsavory way, with "running a
revolution" on the West Side of Chicago. This interview, in particular, and several others wherein the WSO men found their words
and thoughts incompletely and inaccurately reported, reinforced
strong hostilities already felt against the "white press."

At a WSO staff meeting the next day a strategy was adopted to
counteract the alleged misrepresentation of events in the media.
Already a few people had come into WSO to give to reporters (or to
anyone who would listen) their accounts of the police action during
the two nights of rioting. WSO staff decided that all possible
eye-witness accounts should be collected immediately and presented
at a meeting which was supposed to have been already arranged for
the following day with the Mayor of Chicago and the Governor of the
State. The reports would document grievances against police brutality. Several staff persons and volunteers were sent into the
neighborhood,where the fighting had been most intense, to interview
people who had seen events to which they would testify.

The accounts reveal a response to the police action that is
significantly uniform as to the details of certain incidents and
the feelings of many people regarding the pattern of police behavior.
Excessive force was used indiscriminately against any black who was
suspected, who was less than cooperative, or who was just in the
way. The root feeling was that of hatred against an alien force
which had assaulted the community in the name of law and order.

Most of those interviewed were mothers, some with small children, others with teenaged sons. The reality of their neighborhood
becoming the scene of shooting, clubbing, looting, and destruction
meant to these residents of the community that the police had engaged in acts of repression and aggression far in excess of their
rights as peace officers. A few women admitted that the teenagers
were at fault for their lawless behavior and that stern measures
were necessary to punish the offenders. But no one suggested that
this was what the police action meant. Those who claimed to have
seen acts of vandalism and looting said that the real offenders
were never caught and that the police just lashed out to punish anyone they chose for what was happening. Several neighbors testified
to seeing a young boy who was caught by policemen between the
buildings in a CHA courtyard. He claimed to be on his way home,
but was thrown to the ground by the police and beaten by three of
them at one time. Others told of people on their way home from work
who were beaten as they walked along the street, or as they alighted
from buses. Police forcibly entered houses searching for youths
they had been chasing and proceeded to beat persons in the home who
protested their entry. The police were described as "enjoying"
their chance to beat blacks, of saying that "they had been waiting
for this chance for a long time," of using the most abusive racial
epithets.

The question of whether many of these allegations, or even some
of them, could be substantiated is one kind of issue. But another
is the fact that these allegations express the feelings of a great
many people toward the police, who were supposed to guarantee the

protection of their lives and interests. "They treat us like we were animals, like we are less than dogs, like we are inhuman!" Occasionally someone remarked about a good piece of police work which he had observed. But the remark shows the awareness of an exception which proves the rule. And the rule is: "The police are against us and treat us like animals."

A Meeting of Outside Religious Leaders

Later on Thursday afternoon it became known that Dr. King had called a meeting of clergymen from all over the city at the Shiloh Baptist Church. WSO leaders had mixed reactions to this information. Bob Strom was vigorously opposed to the tactic of bringing a host of collared clergymen, most of them white, into the neighborhood to "pour on oil." Robinson was likewise disdainful, saying that if lots of ministers and nuns insisted on marching around the streets and getting their heads bashed, he was not going to try to keep the people quiet. He felt that the presence of the ministers would be inflammatory because the people were already disgusted at being blamed for the rioting which they thought the police themselves had provoked. However, the meeting was definitely on, and Robinson and Bill Darden eventually went to sit on the platform. Other WSO leaders attended.

There were approximately 150 ministers and nuns at the meeting. Hargraves acted as chairman and interpreted the meeting as a discussion among the clergy as to what ought to be their proper ministry within the situation. He warned against the assumption that they-- the clergy--had come in as ministers where there had been no ministry before. WSO people had been present as ministers of peace throughout the whole riot and had offered their bodies in the cause. But what now were the clergy called upon to do?

Chester Robinson spoke first as a representative of the West Side. He spoke of the riot as being, at present, a "small situation" that could become much bigger. He termed it a

> ...silly situation--the silliest I have ever heard of in all my life, that a riot should start over a little water. But what we have to decide now is how to stop this situation. A march around the neighborhood is no good. A mass meeting is no good. It will only create more confusion. People here are aroused. And they are armed. The police are armed. Innocent people are suffering now because of this. There are more people here that want this stopped. But I have heard that some are going to start it up again. What the police have done is they have brought some Negro killer cops, people who will bust open heads and stomp you in the face. I know some of these people. I am an ex-convict and I have known some of them for twenty years. We must go through the neighborhoods and tell them to keep the children at home. And most important, we must watch the police to see whether they will talk to people before they beat them on the head. I want you to see these things with your own eyes. Not just to let me tell you.

Dr. King spoke briefly, but with great feeling, in response to charges from the Mayor and the Chicago *Sun Times* that he and his movement were responsible for inciting, if not instigating, the riot

on the West Side. King's anger was controlled, but very intense,
as he talked of his encounter with the Mayor on Monday of that week,
of the insensitivity of Daley's response to his pleas for correction
of the police abuse and for provision of adequate recreation facilities in the ghetto. King and his staff were blamed for the fact
that the people's resentment of these things had spilled over into
riot. Dr. King gave credit by name to Chester Robinson, Bill Darden,
and the WSO staff for their leadership in helping to avert a situation far worse than had actually occurred. He acknowledged his
fear of losing his own leadership among the people, because he hadn't
been able to produce a victory for them through nonviolent means.
President Kennedy's dictum was quoted. "Those who would make a
peaceful revolution impossible make a violent revolution inevitable."
Dr. King then said emotionally, "I'm trying desperately to lead a
nonviolent movement. I must say I need some help in getting this
faith across." At this point the audience responded with a long
and emotional expression of support. King repeated Robinson's request that if the ministers and nuns agreed to go into the streets
that night, they should look for specific instances of police insensitivity and brutality, recalling that almost every recent major
urban disturbance stemmed from an alleged misuse of police power.
"On the streets one learns that there is bitterness and hatred of
police. These feelings just didn't come from nowhere," he said.
        After the speeches the floor was thrown open for discussion
of strategy. The suggestion was made that the ministers and nuns
work in teams throughout the neighborhoods, under the direction of
WSO staff persons. All participants would wear WSO buttons and, if
they were not in clerical garb, they should at least stay with a
group clearly identifiable as clergy. One resident of the community
urged that only black ministers walk in the neighborhoods. She
feared that the people's anger was such that they would respect no
white person, regardless of whether or not he was a clergyman. Her
argument did not prevail,and a makeshift organizational plan was
adopted. WSO buttons were "sold" at one dollar each, Hargraves
pointing out that these had served as passports for persons the
night before. WSO headquarters was to be the command post for the
teams of clergy. The clergy were instructed to listen carefully
to the people's grievances and to urge the people to stay inside
their homes.
        As it turned out, the Near West Side was entirely calm that
night. Several teams did go out but most came back and dispersed
before darkness had fallen. Hargraves' observation is that only a
minority of the clergy who attended the meeting actually went out
to the street at all. The rest presumably left the area at once.
        A call came in at about 8:00 p.m. from a black clergyman in
the Lawndale area who reported that trouble had started out there
about three miles west and north of WSO. He asked that some of the
clergy come out to help him talk with the people. At that point,
Kale Williams, a Quaker layman, two collared clergymen, and a pos-
tulant nun went to Lawndale and were present during the worst night
of rioting and fighting that summer. After midnight they returned
to WSO and said that they could accomplish nothing more out there.
        Throughout the night WSO remained a center for persons from
all over the city who came to find out what was happening. By that
time the action had shifted far away from the WSO area, and no one
knew anything very much except what came back in the form of rumor.

At one point there were stories of rioting beginning in the Woodlawn and Oakland communities, and some felt that a general uprising throughout the ghetto was beginning. Word came that Doug Andrews and his associates from ACT had been arrested and charged with conspiracy to commit treason. Hargraves, Crawford, Darden, Clark, and Ed Riddick all drove at once to the police station where Andrews was being held, but they were not allowed to enter the front door, nor were they given any information about the men.

On Friday it was announced that the National Guard would be mobilized to patrol the Lawndale area. At 5:00 p.m., 3,000 guardsmen moved out of the armories in full battle dress with combat equipment including automatic and light mortar weapons. Their operations that night were entirely within the Lawndale and Garfield Park area, and WSO people were largely uninvolved.

Aftermath

The reaction in the WSO area to other civil "disturbances" in Gage Park, Cragin, and other white neighborhoods later in the summer of 1966 is a matter of interest. Police and official action was again an issue, since Robinson and the others felt that the white juveniles involved in the burning of cars, beatings, throwing of bricks, etc., during SCLC's open housing marches in these white communities received no more than "a pat on the ass" from the police, compared to the fierce reaction of the police in dealing with the youth and the crowds in the ghetto. The action in Gage Park was never termed "a riot" by the police or by Mayor Daley. The fears generated in these events were fears of blacks marching rather than of white people rioting. The pressures exerted and the injunctions taken were to control the peaceful black and white marchers, rather than the rioting whites. These distinctions were not lost upon the people in the West Side riot area.

Conclusion

The performance of WSO leaders and members during the serious uprising in their neighborhood provides evidence favorable to Archie Hargraves' conviction that local leadership existed and could be trusted to act in the interests of the people from whom it arose. Not only Dr. King, but the press and even the police knew that WSO represented the people whose neighborhood was being ravaged by nearly uncontrollable civil strife. The means of leadership appropriated by the local leaders were actions which they had practiced in other settings and circumstances.

CHAPTER VI

SPOKESMEN FOR THE COMMUNITY: REPRESENTATIVE ACTIONS

Part of a Larger Movement

When WSO was founded in the summer of 1964, it was a critical period for the civil rights revolution. It was the summer of the Mississippi Summer Project and of the first mass civil rights rally in Soldier Field, Chicago, with Martin Luther King Jr. Birmingham had happened, and Selma was just ahead. It could not have been otherwise than that WSO was conceived as part of "the movement."

Marching with Martin Luther King Jr. at Selma was a profound experience for Darden, Robinson, Strom, and Keating. It occurred at a time when the local staff members were off salary, and there was much feeling of hardship within the organization. The sense of belonging to a movement, rather than just to an organization, was the result of marching in Selma. Robinson became convinced that the importance of the black youth within the movement demanded that WSO begin to work in this hitherto neglected area. The leadership of King and Bevel was authenticated for the men, and the way laid for WSO to accept their presence within the Chicago movement in the months to come.

WSO planned a sympathy march from the West Side to City Hall to take place at the same time as King's march to Montgomery. This was WSO's most successful job of canvassing and rallying. More than 200 marchers assembled in the bitter cold and walked to the Loop, where they were addressed by Hargraves and other movement leaders, such as Daniel Alverez, Lawrence Landry, and Jean Lewis. Most of the marchers were teenagers, and this proved to be the beginning of a WSO program to reach and influence the West Side gangs.

WSO also joined the school protest marches and sit-downs in June of 1965 and interpreted this action later as an example of how *not* to be active. There was some feeling in WSO of having been led astray in this demonstration by the leaders from the Coordinating Council of Community Organization. WSO's exact relationship with CCCO is not chronicled in the early material on WSO. It is known that $1,000 was directed to the CCCO organization budget by the Chicago City Missionary Society, in the name of WSO, presumably as a membership fee. But at the height of the Chicago freedom movement activity in the summer of 1966, Robinson, Darden, and others disclaimed WSO's official affiliation with CCCO, though affirming the leadership of Dr. King.

On February 9, 1966, in the Wednesday evening community meeting, Robinson reported a visit by an unnamed Southern Christian Leadership Conference leader to WSO, asking the organization to sponsor a rally of the unemployed in their community, with Dr. King as the promised speaker. It was to be held in one of the large churches

in the WSO area. Robinson had told the SCLC representative that
he was interested in supporting King, and having him speak to the
people, but *only* if King were willing to support WSO in its welfare union effort.

> We are not going to march around City Hall and sing, "We shall over-
> come." Last summer we marched 'til all the food was burned up. Then
> we came home and there was no food in the house. Now we are demanding
> money to live on. We aren't interested in tearing down the slums [a
> reference to the SCLC "victory over slums" theme]. The slums are the
> only place we have. We would be out in the cold if they tear them
> down. We want to know what they [King and Co.] will do for us and
> our demands. If he will come down here and listen to us, and make
> noise for *our* program, we will have him come down.

> The SCLC representative didn't like to hear that; he argued with me
> for four hours, and then left mad. Then he came back and said it was
> a good idea. So he must have talked with somebody higher up. So I
> think maybe Dr. King *will* come down here. If he does, we are going
> to fill the church with welfare recipients, and that's the same thing
> as the poor. And you middle class preachers and other white folks
> will get seats only if there are some left over. The poor are going
> to talk to *him* and tell *him* about this desperate situation and what
> has to be done.

Dr. King came, to speak and to listen, to a packed meeting held
at WSO headquaters. He referred to WSO as "...the most successful
grassroots, community action organization in America." It was
agreed that SCLC would help WSO establish new centers for handling
welfare grievances. These became the welfare union's locals 3 and
4 in East Garfield Park and Lawndale, respectively. Practically
speaking, it meant that WSO used SCLC office space, equipment, and
materials--including telephones--to carry on its welfare work in
the spring and summer of 1966. Possibly, SCLC foresaw a merging
of staff work in this process, but it was not to happen that way.
The arrangement was a troublesome one for WSO.
   In one instance a SCLC staff contingent took some welfare recipients to the Western District Office in Lawndale and introduced
themselves as the WSO welfare union. They had come to get "justice"
for some welfare clients who had been evicted and were unable to
find suitable housing. This action was undertaken without clearing
with WSO officers, and was carried out in a way that dismayed
Crawford and Darden. In the first place, SCLC had gone to one of
the "friendly" offices of the Welfare Department, where WSO had
its best relations with a district supervisor in charge. They had
refused to give their names as representatives of the clients,
saying that it was "immaterial" to the problem, which was one of
"justice." They had brought a case in which it was not even clear
the welfare department could help, if it would. The woman had
eight children, and no landlord would take them in. Crawford
learned, late in the day, that SCLC was trying a sit-in at the
office, with the woman, her children, a man from the DuBois Clubs,
and several SCLC people. Crawford, Curtis Beard, and I rushed to
the office and set out smoothing things over. The woman was finally
housed (by an act of "trickelation," performed by the case work
supervisor--she lied to the landlord about the number of children),

and the incident was closed. But never again were SCLC people per-
mitted a piece of the welfare union action. Crawford commented
disdainfully that they were "all the time acting crazy, without any
sense," which meant, I think, that they were not interested in or
able to pursue the finer points of welfare union work, but were
capable of wrecking everything in the name of "justice."

The summer open housing marches in Gage Park, Cragin, and
other white neighborhoods included a representation of WSO staff
and loyalists. On those occasions when I was present with the WSO
contingent, I felt as though they were the only visible manifestation of the hard-core unemployed in the demonstrations. It is hard
to tell, of course, where the youngsters who filled the ranks were
from, except those that were clearly college students. But I saw
few, if any, other representations of mature ghetto men at the
rallies and marches.

WSO and the Summit Agreement

A proposed march into Cicero had received much publicity and
discussion among WSO people ever since that white suburb was announced earlier in the summer as the ultimate target of the movement's open housing marches. It was clear that the strategy of the
SCLC staff was to keep Cicero as the big threat, the symbol of
direct confrontation between the freedom movement and the white
reactionary forces. It had been announced as a possible target
for a date in the summer, then postponed, and finally set for Sunday, August 28.

The summit conference on open housing called by the Chicago
Commission on Race and Religion began negotiating the week of
August 12, with the pressure of August 28 clearly in focus. At the
end of the first week there were hints to the press that an accord
might be reached soon, which would be recognized by the movement
as a victory--as a concession for which the Cicero march would be
cancelled or postponed indefinitely.

The rumors or hints of a moratorium on marching before August
28 reached their height in the days before the march. Nevertheless, plans were pushed ahead for the march, including an announced
mass meeting at WSO for Wednesday, August 24, to create enthusiasm
and give instructions for the march. James Bevel came to this
meeting and spoke generally on the significance of the open housing
marches. Archie Hargraves spoke next and declared WSO's intention
of acting out of a new reality--the reality of new creaturehood for
the people of the ghetto who, from that moment on, were living as
free citizens of an open city. Cicero on Sunday was to be the
public statement of that new reality. Robinson curiously had little
to say about Cicero, though he spoke for over an hour. But he
affirmed the significance of Cicero as a target for black demonstrations in a few sentences.

Cicero is important. Three days before James Meredith got shot
down in Mississippi, a Negro from Chicago [Jerome Huey, a black
teenager from Hyde Park High School] got beaten in the head. His
eyes were beaten out, and he was laying on the sidewalk. But then
people said, "Let's march in Mississippi because Meredith got some
buckshots in his behind." But a young teenager looking for a job

was beaten to death in Cicero. So I decided right then and there
I'll never march in the South. But I'll go marching into Cicero.

In the end no actual organization took place at the community meeting
relative to the Cicero march, a fact which some of the staff members
found disturbing.
     On Friday afternoon of that week, the news story broke that
accord had been reached by King and his forces with the Mayor and
the realty interests, with the church representatives on the
"summit conference" as validating witnesses. King announced
simultaneously that the Cicero march was "postponed indefinitely."
That evening a mass rally had been scheduled in Lawndale at the
Stone Baptist Temple for the particular purpose of drawing attention
to the work of the tenants' union program of strikes against landlords. John Crawford was scheduled to appear on behalf on the welfare union program in Lawndale. King had agreed to be there to
lend support. When the agreements were signed that afternoon, the
SCLC leadership decided that the meeting ought to be a victory rally
as well. There was dissension that evening, even on the platform,
as it was being decided finally who was going to speak on what.
Could a tenants' union and a rent strike program against landlords
be melded effectively with a celebration of accords with realty
interests and the political powers? King did speak, and Meredith
Gilbert from the tenants' union as well. But the real dissent broke
out following the meeting, as Chester Robinson announced to a news
conference that WSO did *not* affirm the agreements of the summit conference, because they included nothing for the poor people WSO represented, and because the poor themselves, or their representatives,
had never been consulted. WSO would march on Cicero August 28.

Managing Conflict

     One of the WSO loyalists, with a fast pen, composed an editor-
ial statement which Robinson phoned to Pat Stock, *West Side Torch*
editor, who, at that moment was putting the paper to bed at the
printing offices in Woodlawn. The paper appeared in the morning
with the following editorial, signed by Chester Robinson, on the
front page:

"BIG SELL OUT"

Who is surprised? Not us, say the grass roots. The so-called leaders
of the "Freedom Movement" have again proven that they are not representative of the poor or even the not-so-poor.

The betrayal at the Palmer House is a sickening example of the leadership of those whom the power structure has chosen as our representatives.

No freedom will ever come to the black people of Chicago (or any
other place) as long as they fight by rules laid down by Mr. Charlie.

     Saturday morning the metropolitan press carried as headline
news WSO's rejection and promise to march. The Cicero march would
be organized at WSO and would include Student Non-violent Coordinating

Committee, the Oakland Committee for Community Improvement, and the Deacons for Defense and Justice. The Chicago Chapter of the Council on Racial Equality (CORE) made known its interest in a march also, and the dissidents agreed to meet Saturday noon at WSO to plan the strategy.

The Saturday morning scene at WSO was reminiscent of the days during the rioting earlier in the summer. The place was frantic with telephones ringing, reporters and cameramen about, emissaries arriving and leaving, and hosts of persons gravitating to the place to learn what action was in store. In the midst of this Chester Robinson and several of the WSO loyalists sat at the front of the office placidly watching a Hollywood film on TV ignoring as much of the confusion as possible. At about 11:00 a.m., a number of pressmen responded to the rumor that a conference was about to be held by Robinson.

In the midst of this incredible scene, with reporters from UPI, local TV, and several national newspapers trying to pry a statement from Chester Robinson as to whether WSO would indeed march into Cicero the next day, the WSO director began conducting a scheduled interview with a Mr. Koslo, representing the Stern Family Fund. Koslo had the assignment of preparing a report for his foundation board which was to decide whether or not to renew the WSO grant in aid for a second year. A sum of $10,000 was at issue (two-fifths of the WSO yearly budget). The interview was held around the small communion table given to WSO by the Chicago City Missionary Society from the furnishings of the defunct Cragin Congregational Church. People were swarming all over the room. Koslo accepted good-naturedly the unusual situation for an important interview and asked Robinson if WSO considered itself to be a militant organization. The reply was as follows:

> Actually we are not direct action oriented. I don't mean we don't go into action, but we don't do it very often. We are involved in processing grievances, getting people jobs and food. Lots of people don't see us this way. They call us militant. We go into public offices on the side of the law. They know we have the law on our side. The Cicero march is something we wanted to do when Jerome Huey got killed trying to get a job earning his way through college. Cicero has been closed for years. We can't go for a walk there, go into a restaurant, or go into a tavern. Negroes who walk there always are in danger. We need to dramatize the fact that Negroes in Cicero need protection. That's why we want to march.

About 12:30 the representatives from the various dissident organizations opposing the summit agreement arrived at WSO, and the room was cleared for the strategy meeting. This put the entire press corps, which now included TV people with their paraphernalia, out on the sidewalk in front of WSO for what proved to be a very long, hot session of waiting.

Hargraves had been asked to draw up a statement declaring WSO's reasons for insisting on the Cicero march. The statement contained references to the Huey murder, the sunrise-to-sundown restrictions upon blacks who worked in Cicero, the indignity of being cordonned off from a sector of the metropolitan community, as if blacks were a lesser form of humanity. The grounds for rejecting the summit agreement were also interpreted, using the analogy of the airline

mechanics' rank and file, who earlier in the summer had rejected
the negotiations made on their behalf with the airline industry.
The main grievances were the lack of concern with the gut issues
that affected the rank and file WSO constituents. The statement
made a guarded reaffirmation of the leadership of King and his staff,
but upheld the right of dissent in this instance.

The meeting was chaired by Robinson and began with a discussion
of what was and was not an issue for decision. A WSO staff person
signalled the presence of some disagreement on the matter by saying,
"Maybe I haven't marched before because I am a coward. But I in-
tend to march to Cicero when it can be done without the result being
that we just get arrested and thrown in jail." No permit to march
to Cicero had been obtained, and there was doubt one could be applied for before Sunday, the next day. The CORE representative declared he didn't want a discussion of whether or not the march was
to go on; that was already settled. But he did want to discuss the
timing. He had planned a march in Cicero for September 4, the following Sunday. Did the others want to join his plans? At that
point it was decided that anyone opposed to marching in Cicero would
not be allowed to remain in the meeting, and each person present
was asked for a commitment. One SCLC leader, a local Chicago pastor,
declared his willingness to march in Cicero, but he was interested
in certain conditions being met. First, he did not want to see disunity among the civil rights forces. He was told in response that
disunity existed already, and this was only making it plain. Second,
he raised as a condition of marching anywhere the need for a definite
target. To this the statement of Hargraves was read and agreed upon.

Finally a vote was taken, on the suggestion of CORE, to declare
the march definitely on for September 4, eight days ahead. The
vote was fourteen in favor, nine against. All who voted were again
committed to march, whether or not they opposed the tactic. The
WSO contingent was clearly split. Finally the group adjourned to
meet the press outside on the sidewalk with the announcement of a
joint march for September 4.

On August 28 another meeting was held with CORE at WSO, at
which time much dissension was expressed, and WSO announced its
prerogative to pull out of the march entirely, if it saw fit. The
WSO staff met later and indeed decided that it would withdraw from
the coalition planning to march in Cicero. However, they determined
to make no public announcement of the decision, but to allow Dr.
King to make an advertised intervention in the dispute and take
public credit for resolving the difficulty. The further implication
would be that Dr. King and his leadership were acceding to WSO demands for better representation and attention to the grievances of
the poor.

This strategy was nearly sabotaged by a publicized report from
a CCMS board official who was very much involved in the summit
agreement, that the Board was now going to review some of its commitments to community organizations like WSO, in reprisal for their
independent action against the summit accords. WSO again felt the
challenge of appearing to be controlled by white business and church
interests downtown. Therefore, as of Tuesday, August 30, the march
was on again. The general unhappiness around WSO with this course
of events led to the expectation that something would certainly happen
to make unlikely WSO participation in the Cicero march. It remained
for the Wednesday night community meeting at WSO to deal with the
issue.

Identifying the Issues and Managing the Consensus

On Wednesday evening, August 31, Mrs. Greta Edwards, a WSO loyalist, appeared with a list of specific grievances which WSO was making against the power structures in the city, and which represented the "authentic needs" of the poor who allegedly had been bypassed in the summit agreement. This list had been worked out by Mrs. Edwards and Chester Robinson. The strategy was to ask the community whether this list did, or did not, express their *real* grievances, and whether they would vote to have WSO withdraw from the march, provided Dr. King would agree personally to pursue these specific demands with the power structure. The list included the following items:

1. The Chicago Housing Authority should hire more people from the near west side for CHA jobs.
2. The maximum level of income allowable for remaining in CHA housing should be raised.
3. The issue of income earned by minors in the family should be resolved so that CHA families were not penalized (by having to move out) when their children were able to earn.
4. The elimination of the five-day rental notice--i.e., the requirement that rents must be paid within five days of the beginning of each month, or else a five dollar penalty is assessed.
5. Clarification of eviction policies, with a ninety-day notice mandatory.
6. A flat rent should be established, with breaks given to the senior citizens and those on Social Security to allow more than one bed per apartment. That is to say, rent for aged persons sharing an apartment should be a flat amount, not geared to the number of beds in each.
7. All interest accruing from security deposits with CHA should be returned to the tenants each year by check.
8. Damages should not be charged to the tenant for damages incurred without his knowledge.
9. The maximum use of utilities should be raised for each building.
10. The CHA should adhere to the state code with respect to the size of apartments and maintenance within the apartments.
11. All apartments should be equipped with garbage cans or disposals.
12. Contracts for the training of finishers and other skilled workmen should be obtained through OEO with the provision that west siders would be trained for these jobs.
13. There should be regular three-month extermination services.
14. There should be public washrooms on the first floors of buildings.
15. The building residents should determine whether the public rooms and social facilities in the buildings should be given over to the use of agencies, such as Welfare.
16. Dangerous concrete playgrounds should be eliminated and a softer, less dangerous material used.
17. A workable security system should be installed in all buildings.
18. There should be operators on the elevators at all times.
19. For those on welfare, there should be an elimination of the ceilings for welfare supported housing.

20. Welfare recipients should be informed of their rights to with-
    hold rents from slum landlords.
21. When welfare tenants request the public aid authorities to with-
    hold rent from slum landlords, there should be action on the
    request within 48 hours.
22. Public Aid recipients should have unhindered access to housing
    anywhere in Cook County.
23. Fifty families from WSO's welfare unions should be relocated
    immediately in adequate housing as a sign of the intentions of
    the city to open housing for the poor.
24. Homemakers' allowances for recipients should be liberalized.
25. The utility allowance should be removed, and the amount paid in
    cash to the recipients.

When these demands were read, Bill Darden and Chester Robinson
each spoke at length about the reasons why these grievances were
selected as a bargaining position for WSO.   Robinson's statement
is included here as an excellent example of his ability, with humor
and conviction, to express his position, and to exact "agreement."

Now every Negro in here tonight, if they say, "Now you go out in
Cicero right now, move in, and pay twenty-five dollars per month for
rent," you would just go on home, turn on your TV, sit down and smoke
a cigarette--'cause you ain't about to go out there--not to Gage
Park, or to any other park. They have created not only hate in that
community, but fear in the Negro community, because you know what
you got waiting for you. And that's that, if you don't go out there
in strength. 'Cause you sure ain't going out there by yourself.

Now what do we do? Now they say when we get all of this [the summit agreement] they going to open up all of the city. Now, I don't
see no *doors* on the city anywhere. I don't know that they mean by
opening up the city. Let all them middle class people move where
they want to move. Now I told my mother--we just bought a home--I
told her, "Now wait, when they open up this city we can get a home
in a white neighborhood for half that amount of money." She said,
"All right." But when she saw all this on television, she said,
"I'm going to put my money on *this* building, because I am not going
to put up with all that stuff. All I want to do is live." There is
lots of people that feel that way. The point is they are misusing
us in our own ghetto. Right here. Let's fix things right here first.

Now if I made $200 per week, like some of those folks in Gage Park
has, and the rent is $90 per month, then I'd have a whole lot of
money to play with. I could put some of it in the bank. But you
can't make that much and stay in CHA. Now that don't make no sense.
And you can't grow grass there no way. But they say *we* dug up the
grass....But you know, people will say anything to indoctrinate you.

But I don't believe in philosophies, and doctrination. All that
stuff can go. Jesus had that fish and that bread. You know, he did
a whole lot with that. And I believe we can do a whole lot with our
basic problems. But if we ain't got no jobs, we ain't going to be
able to *live*, much less move out anywhere. If you can't pay the
rent, you are going to be put out in the streets, and here they [CHA]
is charging you if you is five days late. And that automatic five

dollars every month goes to CHA. Your check don't come 'til the
tenth, and the rent is due on the third. And that automatic five
dollars every month goes to CHA. They are taking your money. You
put up a sixty dollar [security] deposit. Do you realize how many
pay that? You just add it up. Where is that money at? Who gets
the interest on that? That's *your* money, not theirs. This has got
to be looked into. They is just taking your money. Now, the Robert
Brooks homes is twenty-four years old. If that door breaks, and you
can't open it up, *you* got to pay for it. I know *we* do. Now that
door is twenty-four years old. They know you got to pay for something. They are just taking your money. I read a report in the
paper where CHA is making money! They oughta be making money! More
than the bank! And when you move out of the project they always
find an excuse to keep that sixty dollars deposit. I ain't heard
nobody got it back yet. All these demands are important.

They always say, "You is living off us." But I'm a taxpayer. When
I get a check for seventy-five dollars, twelve dollars is gone from
it just like that. For whom? I don't like to walk down hard streets.
I like to walk down a dirt road. Who are those highways for? If
your house burned down tonight, it would just stay burned down. But
if a hole opens up in one of those expressways, they would have it
fixed up in one hour. They care more about bricks than they do about
people. That's a fact. They don't want them bankers to have a bumpy
road going back and forth. They even made it so good they have all
the streets going one way now. They said it was too crowded. They
know we ain't driving nothing. We left our mules down in Mississippi.

*What I don't like is people in high places always saying what some-
body needs! They's always saying it.* "Those old colored folks need
recreation facilities, ping pong tables, checkers." And your son
grows up this skinny. He can't get no exercise. How do they know
what we need? And they ain't never been into this community. They
don't even know what the streets look like. It tickles me, how some
of these white folks call me up and say, "I want to talk with you,
Mr. Robinson." They live in Chicago. And I say, "Well, come down
to 1537 Roosevelt Road." And they say, "Well, where is that at?"
They don't even know you exist. One of our students last year, his
wife came with him. And they went over to that area there [west of
Ashland] and she cried like a baby. She said she didn't know those
conditions existed. "I didn't think people lived like that." When
one of the students came to live in from Earlham College, he went
over to one of the ADC recipient's house, he walked back in here,
and his eyes had stayed red. He said he didn't know. I didn't have
no pity for him. I wasn't sorry for him 'cause he was crying. I
said to him, "You is an educated fool! You might know how to read
and write, and add, but you don't know what is going on in the world
you are living in. You don't even know whether someone is here to
destroy you or not. You are walking in this neighborhood where there
are some colored people liable to cut your face, and you don't even
know why." That's right. If I go out into a white neighborhood, I
know why they is going to cut my throat.

So we are talking about these agreements as phony for one reason--
they left us out. They got a housing agreement in there. This is
just one of 200 failures they could have put down. They haven't got

nothing in here about a piece of bread, a glass of milk, and a job.
Just long words that we don't understand. If they are that far apart
from us, then somebody gon' to have to meet with them. 'Cause when
we go to Cicero--we have to go. There ain't no question about that,
'cause Cicero is just like the Berlin Wall. It's got to be knocked
down....There is one way *we* can do it. Now that man over there across
the street [in the supermarket] now he don't live over there. Now
one way to make him deal with the issue is to say, "Well, you got a
home in Cicero, but you got a store across the street. Now we can't
get to Cicero, so you can't come here to your store." That ain't no
threat, talk about shooting him or cutting him, you know. Somebody
might do it, but this is not what I'm talkin' about. Negroes spend
billions of dollars per year. We got buying power. We got political
power.

What I call a sell-out is when you get to a table, and you sit down
with somebody and you say, "*My* people needs this. *My* people needs
that." I don't think anybody here seen a thing in those agreements
that will benefit you. So evidently somebody down there didn't know
what their people needed. So they hadn't any business down there
negotiating, saying, "My people nothing." The people have to speak
sometime. I'm not talking about Dr. King 'cause Dr. King really does
all the preaching and hard work. But there was a lot of people down
there just playing games, playing games with your lives. They want
to be top dog. They want to have those twenty to thirty thousand
dollar a year jobs. And I was there. And I seen what went down.
They is cheating on us. They want us to walk, march, holler, and
sing everything, and everybody else will get the gravy. And we will
still be right here, walking, marching, hollering, and singing.

So it is up to us to say, "Well, we don't want *that* much. Maybe if
we are getting $280 a month on welfare, give us $300 instead." Or
something like *that*. We have got to ask for something. The paper
said, "The movement did this." The movement ain't done nothing. They
had a bunch of Catholic priests, Episcopalians, the Archbishop, Mayor
Daley, and all those millionaires. They say, "We are trying to help
the poor people." You had over a billion dollars worth of men in
there. If they wanted to help, they could have given you half of
that billion dollars. But they are trying to get the glory, you know.
"I'm the great humanitarian." You know they ain't nothing. Big
people fight over little people. That is how wars start. They don't
start over money. Who is going to control these folks, and who is
going to control the other folks? And they fight to see who is going
to control, who has the power. And here *you* got all the power. So
we are going to control *ourselves*. And you [down there] aren't
nothing. We are going to control ourselves. And you got to go.

So we got to do something right now. Now, I'm going to see Dr. King
in the morning. And I got to tell him something. And what I want
now is a consensus. If he meets these demands, if he agrees to take
these demands to the city and get an "okay," then I don't think we
should march. But if he don't, I think we should march to Cicero
every day. So this is the kind of consensus we want. If everybody
thinks this is a good proposal for the time being--we are going to
start coming up with one every month now--[diversion]. See, in WSO
when we have a meeting we always have ten or fifteen white folks, and

the rest of us is colored. That was what surprised Dr. King the last
time he spoke here. He was looking around trying to find the white
liberals. This is important, 'cause the paper always says [about the
movement] "Don't worry about them cause most of them is white liberals
trying to help the poor colored folks." But in WSO they got colored
folks *teaching* white liberals. [This brought down the house.] This
is important for us to realize this. They say we is prejudiced and
hates white folks. They even says how much we hates them. I ain't in
that. But one thing is sure about WSO--we got all kinds in here....

Now I want everybody who is in favor of this agreement of having a
meeting [with Dr. King] and trying to get somebody to meet these demands to raise their hands. [Show] That's good. I ain't going to
ask who is opposed, 'cause I don't want to hate nobody. Some people
going to call us sell-outs, too. But they ain't going to process no
case, or get nobody into CHA. They ain't going to do nothing else.
See, they don't see these little babies running 'round here begging
and hungry.

Now we might not march. But one thing has to be positive--and I want
everybody to realize this--we have to be sure of ourselves when we say
that. If they don't meet the poor people's demands, we are just going
to march--period. I got some neighborhoods in mind that Dr. King
hasn't heard of....if we get lucky, we might just go up there and set
in Mayor Daley's office and have some lunch or something. Just do
something--anything. When they see all the elderly women, or that
woman over there with a baby and a milk bottle, just sitting down
there, they ain't going to hit a hole in their heads. Oh, they will
hit those students with the long hair all the way down their backs....
They'll bother them. But the mothers, the fathers, the people who
are suffering--see, they know who is suffering, and who isn't. Those
college students with the holes in their pants, they got money. They
just want to act crazy or something--or just to save their money. I
don't know what they are doing. But when we go somewhere, we are
going to look clean. Put on the Sunday dress, and just sit there,
or go on the picket line. But they know us.

But one thing they don't know about us... and that is that we are
coming together. They are beginning to find out. They can call us
all the names in the world. But they don't know that we are coming
together. And that we have started to think together. . . .that we
are realizing that all of our problems are right there in one. We
all have one problem, and can't nobody on the face of the earth can
solve this problem but yourself. Believe me what I tell you, if you
aren't goin' to do nothing, ain't nobody goin' to do nothing for you.
[Applause]

Reconciliation

On Thursday, September 1, Dr. King and three others arrived at
WSO at 11:30 a.m. for a meeting with the community organization.
The entire WSO staff was present, including volunteers like myself.
Chester Robinson opened the meeting with a good statement about why
they were in disaccord with the summit agreement, and he presented
the list of demands adopted by the organization to King and Andrew

Young. He said he felt like the ghetto poor people had not been
listened to at all by the negotiators and that the agreements had
nothing in them that they could regard as victories for the poor.
    Dr. King replied that he was very interested to know what the
people Chester worked with had as their grievances. He said that
he realized now that some mistakes had been made in the negotiating
procedures, that more specifics should have been included in what
was agreed to, and that Chester should have been in on the negotiating. However, he felt bothered by the charge that there had been
a sell-out by him. He said he was willing to acknowledge mistakes
he had made, but not that he had ever sold out, because that would
be a reflection upon his integrity. He pointed out that he was
committed to the movement in Chicago, even to the giving of his
life, if needed, and that he had received offers of money to leave
Chicago. Mayor Daley had sent an emissary directly to him offering
to appoint a committee on integration in Chicago that would include
one-half of King's people and one-half of Daley's, but on the condition that King would leave. King rejected these offers which,
he said, *would* have constituted a sell-out, if he had taken them.
King was very restrained but firm on this point, and Archie Hargraves interrupted to state that WSO had decided together that they
would like to offer their apologies to Dr. King for any "intemperate"
remarks that had been made in the course of the recent events. Dr.
King said that he would accept the apology knowing that it was sin-
cerely offered.
    Andrew Young then went into some of the specifics of the grie-
vances, pointing out that they could be presented naturally as explicit exemplifications of certain general principles which the
conferees had already agreed upon. He said, in effect, that some
of these had already been discussed in negotiation, and he was sure
that such things as flat rents for CHA, open housing efforts for
welfare, proper security and custodial services, etc., were going
to be insisted upon, and granted. Then he asked Chester if he were
going on the CCCO retreat with him and his staff scheduled to begin
that afternoon in Ottawa, Illinois. Archie and Chester agreed they
would go along, a sign to all that WSO was "on board" again.
    Dr. King went on to state that he felt unsure, at present, ex-
actly what major attack to launch, now that the first round of the
fifteen round battle had been won. Perhaps it ought to be the
employment problem, and he noted with appreciation the demand that
employment matters having to do with CHA and urban renewal were
specified by WSO. He mentioned the attempt to join with unions in
helping put Negro employees in stores, such as Saks Fifth Avenue.
But, he said, he was about to conclude that the welfare issue was
the most critical one for the movement to tackle at once, on a wide
scale, and for this WSO was crucial for their plans, since WSO had
all the know-how and expertise on what to do and how to push.
    Further discussion of the issues opened up the question of the
Coordinating Council of Community Organizations as a proper agent for
the movement, and Robinson and Darden expressed sharp disagreement
and disapproval of CCCO leadership. Robinson said, "When you set
up a bank you don't put Jesse James in as one of the cashiers."
WSO had evidence, he claimed, that CCCO had persons in its leadership who were willing to operate in cahoots with the power structures, the very people WSO and the movement were supposedly fighting.
King expressed surprise at this, and Bill Darden said, "There's

lots of things you don't know about this here situation." King apologized for his naivete and said he was open to a complete re-structuring of CCCO, or any other umbrella agency, but that up until now he was bound to them by the fact that CCCO had issued the invitation for SCLC to come to Chicago.

Robinson then asked for clarification on one further point, the issue of Cicero itself. He told of the meaning of Cicero to the people of the West Side and asked whether Dr. King would even-tually be willing to go into that fortress of segregation. King responded affirmatively, saying they would *have* to go to Cicero. The real question was *when* to go to effect the greatest good. Chester accepted this condition, and it was agreed that WSO would *not* march on September 4 into Cicero.

Next the decision was made as to how the press was to be approached with all of this: King was to make the initial state-ment regarding the WSO grievances which were not made part of the negotiations at the summit, and Chester Robinson was to announce and explain that WSO would not march into Cicero after all on September 4.

There were marches into Cicero in the late summer of 1966 led by CORE and joined by a few other sympathizers, but WSO was not in-volved.

Conclusion

There are conflicting interpretations of why WSO acted as it did in challenging the leadership of Dr. King and the coalition of movement and establishment figures who sought to end the summer of conflict in 1966. Personal jealousies and animosity which obscured the larger goal can be offered as explanations. But the data show other dynamics at work -- the consistent intention of WSO to main-tain cordial but tenuous relations with the larger movement in Chicago, an insistence upon its own methods of welfare activism (based upon WSO's hard-won right of access to the welfare district offices where it could exercise judicious clout), and a sense of its representative responsibility to the people of its own neigh-borhood who were not making strategy with King nor being assisted in their urgent needs. WSO resisted absorption by the well-publicized local "movement" structure, and resisted being drawn off into a counter-movement of persons with no access to power of any sort, except the intimidation of peace authorities. As will be discussed in the concluding chapter, WSO's representative power came from its sense of performing the fitting action at the appro-priate time, an ideological strategy.

CHAPTER VII

A REINTERPRETATION OF THE

IDEOLOGY OF DEVIANCE

> The function of an ideology is to
> make an autonomous politics pos-
> sible by providing the authorita-
> tive concepts that render it mean-
> ingful, the suasive images by
> means of which it can be sensibly
> grasped.
>
> Clifford Geertz

Introduction

The reader will remember my claim at the outset of this study
that the actions of the West Side Organization may be understood as
countering a pervasive ideology in American culture. According to
that ideology, people who are restive and alienated within circumstances of chronic poverty are perceived and described in terms of
deviance from the "normal" or even the "natural." Within this view,
when the social conduct of such persons is attributed to their own
acts of will, they will be understood as "revolutionaries" (if they
constitute a sizeable, organized group), as members of a "gang" (if
they are few), or as "criminals" (if they are considered as individuals). These terms (and others of the same family type) associate
with one another in an ideological context that connotes "bad
character." If, however, there exists a more enlightened awareness of the social and economic conditions of those who are alienated,
the ideology of deviance allows for explanations of their conduct
which suggest that their actions are not willed by them, but caused
in them. The correlative images are "pathological," "victims of
mass hysteria" and "sick individuals." Although the images are
different, they are still associated within an ambiance of deviance.
It is hardly necessary to point out that this ideological pic-
ture is too crudely formulated to admit more sophisticated understandings of alienated and dissatisfied people, some of which may
indeed escape the ideological framework of deviance. But an ideological shorthand not unlike that just sketched was operative in
the public media, in the responses of civic groups, agencies,
churches, and in the attitude of individuals who encountered WSO
from outside its community, or from some other cultural and social
location within it.
The actions of WSO, expressed through their leadership, and
described in this study, were strategies directed against this reg-
nant and dehumanizing ideology. In terms of meaning, the symbols
of "revolutionaries," "gang members," "criminals," did not compre-

hend either the motivational structure of the actors, or the character of the association created and sustained in the actions I have
recounted. Nor did the symbols reflecting a social pathology,
visited upon these persons as actors and members of a voluntary
association, provide a persuasive set of images in which the reality
could be grasped. The ideology of deviance, with its various re-
finements, simply does not account for the facts which emerged in
the experiences described herein.

The concept of ideology is, of course, associated classically
with analyses of power relationships in society. Concentrating,
as I do here, on meanings being denied or shifted in order to fit
the realities of personal and communal existence does not obviate
the fact that structures of meaning also represent structures of
dominance in society. Shifts in meaning, which constitute new
occasions of communication among parties, also reconstitute structures of power relation in the society. Power is used here in the
sense of a capacity to attain some goal or result which is dependent
upon the agency of others.

Whether personal agency is a factor which is ever completely
obliterated in an enactment of power relationship, i.e., through
the exercise of sheer material force, is a question of philosophical
importance related to the nature of human action and agency. Power
may, of course, be used more restrictively, to refer simply to the
ability to prevail in any conflict of interests. For the purposes
of this study, however, agency is assumed to be essential to action,
and therefore a communication of meaning is also an act of suasion
in which there is an attempt to accomplish some purpose which is
dependent upon the agency of another.

The reformation of an ideology of deviance in WSO is, in this
sense, a study of attempts to reconstitute power relationships in
an urban society. The fact that the shifts in power relationship
perceived emerging in this study are tentative at best, and certainly
not measureable by any standard of magnitude, should not, I think,
preclude our interest in the relationship between the reconstitution
of meanings in the cultural sphere and changes in the capacities of
persons and groups to utilize the agency of others in their projects.

In this study I am also charting an attempt to reconstitute
the moral meaning that ideological symbols convey. Within the
ideology of deviance there are distinctions in moral tone between
those symbols which attribute bad character to actors and those
which eschew moralistic judgments in favor of interpretations of
social pathology. But the moral valence of either form of appel-
lation within the ideology of deviance works against the capacity
to articulate a sense of right counterbalanced by a sense of obligation in the motivational structure of actors who must view themselves in these images.

Individuals who are morally "bad" or characteriologically
"sick" cannot find for themselves, within the expectations and
opportunities of society, an endowment of reciprocal rights and
obligations with which to make their moral decisions. To put it
differently, persons who are morally free and characteriologically
whole can find that their society provides them with good
reasons for choosing the good, and good roles within which to enact
the good, for themselves and others at the same time.

The ideology of deviance, including its social liberal variant,
in which deviant action is never simply "their fault," is an impov-

erishment of the moral structure of right and obligation, against which the resourceful actor *must* protest. One may claim justifiably that economic and political structures provide few good reasons for actors to choose the good, or good roles for actors to enact the good, for themselves or for others. However, to avoid becoming part of the pathological problem itself, to prevent the generation of self-fulfilling prophecies regarding the incapacities of persons to act in their own self-interest, one must recognize and honor the free and responsible judgments of those who suffer the burdens, and who have associated voluntarily to interpret these realities to one another. Only in this way can the actor transcend the determinisms of an unjust order.

Social analysis from the perspective of the actor is not simply a romantic ideal. *It is an essential condition for understanding the moral significance of persons experiencing the reality of their own freedom and humanity, the reality of determinisms transcended through the reconstitution of meaning and power in the social sphere.*

Our task is to understand the actions of WSO as rhetorical strategies, aimed at particular audiences, for the purpose of creating new interpretations of real situations. The leadership of WSO acted in many instances to shift meanings, with their moral weight and their political implications, where those meanings did not fit the reality of life within their community, and within their organization which, they claimed, was a microcosm of the "real" community of the Near West Side. Their "audiences" were numerous and varied--close associates of the leaders within WSO and its support groups, street people of the community, welfare families, "respectable" people of the Near West Side. They included also a group of business figures downtown who were alternatively hesitant, intrigued, and outraged by the organization with which they found themselves involved. And there were others--press, black militants, mainline civil rights organizations, police and judiciary, the welfare bureaucracy, and city agencies. There were occasions, too, when the appeal of the action was directed to the inner selfhood of those who engaged in it, and perhaps even to something, someone, perceived as the Ultimate Reality, the final source of appeal.

A full accounting of the motives would remain sensitive to each of these different audiences to whom the persuasion was addressed, though, in this study, there is very little data on which to interpret the psychological dynamics of the actors. However, to understand the rhetorical significance of public actions it is not necessary to probe for the conscious intentions of the actors, nor to presume that what can be observed and interpreted even corresponds to a willful project of any single person. We can go some distance, at least, by discriminating as carefully as possible among the various publics with whom WSO was making its case, the symbols it attacked, or reinterpreted, and the strategies it invented, or found at hand, to negotiate new meanings and new relations on the Near West Side.

Countering the Symbols of Indignity

The initial strategy of this group of young men upon entering the public sphere was to challenge "the given." This may be seen

clearly in the designation of Centennial Laundry as a target. For
nearly two months, prior to the first conversation that Keating and
others had with Chester Robinson, when he identified Centennial as
an appropriate focus of action, WSO had been conducting a different
type of action, namely, looking for specific job opportunities to
offer to the men (and to the women, as well) who came through its
doors. Many businesses and industries, in and out of the neighborhood, had been solicited for jobs, with WSO men carrying the story
of a new type of group forming in the ghetto. WSO was not intended
to be a job agency, as such, but a committed community of men helping
one another to make it in the tough area of finding and keeping jobs.
Indeed this had been the meaning of Keating's first call at Centennial Laundry, in which he, a white man, had been received by the
management with a heartening show of interest.
    But when Robinson came into the group, the tactic shifted
radically. The chief issue for WSO became not the problem of unemployment, but the problem of *dignified* employment. Black men and
women could find work at Centennial, but not dignified work--work
for which the standard of reward for loyalty and enterprise was a
middle class income and visible responsibility. Thereafter, in
everything else that WSO was to undertake in the area of employment,
this became the fundamental point of the action.
    In 1964, WSO was reluctant to channel black men into jobs paying
lower than $2.00 per hour, for that would mean, as Robinson often
interpreted it, that they were working for less than a subsistence
wage, which was the same thing as being a slave. It would be better
to live off the "capital" accrued to this country through the labor
of poor people in the past and now dispensed in paltry dribbles in
the form of welfare, than to continue toiling in a servile occupa-
tion, which held no chance for meaningful advancement, no opportunity
for increased responsibility. Thus there could be no shame in
taking what had been already earned through the long years of exploitation of black labor, stretching back into the period of legal
slavery. Simply to obtain jobs on Centennial's "plantation" was to
revert willingly to subjugation within the white man's economy.
    In the modern industrial society it is largely within the power
of the economic institutions to convey or deny essential assurances
of worth. Robinson recognized this from the outset and insisted
upon it as the condition of his participation in the organization.
Centennial's blacks were chattel who were, literally and figuratively,
doing the white man's dirty laundry, though "gainfully employed" and
"legally protected" in their rights by a union. The goals which WSO
demanded--eight black men in charge of delivery routes, to be *chosen*
by WSO, as the employment agent for the firm--were precisely those
accessions which Centennial could not make and still retain its
categorical exclusion of blacks from status and honor within the
system. Centennial became the representative context in which to
probe for the weaknesses in an ideological screen, exposing them
for public scrutiny. At the same time the action against Centennial
enabled the young men of the community to exercise leadership roles
before various audiences. When the audience then addressed con-
sisted of the poor of the neighborhood *and* the liberals of the supporting institutions (especially the churches), the hope was that
they would coalesce in a new polity.
    Centennial's fitness for the role of representative symbol of
"the given" is nicely exemplified by its standards for employment.

These were used, not to exclude all black persons who came to the laundry seeking jobs (since there were many already working in menial jobs within the plant who could *not* meet Centennial's formal requirements), but to exclude them from job categories with access to increasing responsibility and pay.   In other words, the standards were a device to ensure a ready supply of cheap labor among persons who were not in compliance and were therefore dependent upon the willingness of management to keep them employed.

In themselves the standards seem not unreasonable, given the ideological basis for understanding the poor for whom they were established.   The standards were those of a "fair employment firm," which required that persons hired to engage in cash transactions be bondable, with no criminal records.   They must show a continuous and satisfactory employment record, proof that they were living within the bonds of respectable marriage, and they must be able to pass a lie detector test on the facts stated in their employment applications.   It was demanded furthermore that the applicant be a high school graduate with a diploma, not a certificate of equivalent education.   How did WSO's rhetorical strategy, through its attack on Centennial Laundry counter, shift, or otherwise transvalue the terms of these requirements?

The standards of educational fitness were attacked within the organization in a variety of ways.   In the public meetings the men sometimes referred openly to the poor educational opportunities of their youth.   In a sense this was an acceptance of the "victimized" image which operated within the ideology of deviance they were opposing.   Although the rhetoric of the Black Power challenges to public education was not yet being heard around WSO, the problem they faced in being "poorly educated" was explained by them, in part, by the racism they had encountered in the public schools and by the economic deprivations they suffered as children.   John Crawford, in particular, remembered certain teachers who made him feel that he, as a black child, had something deficient in his makeup.   He spoke of being too hungry and too poorly clothed to feel confident in school, to learn quickly, or want to stay there longer than the required minimum.

More positively, the leaders sought to provide public evidence of their own educational achievements beyond the formal school years and in the more demanding school of experience.   Several of the WSO leaders became intellectually alive after leaving school, in the army where several finished their high school requirements, or in contact with movement people who directed their reading in Afro-American history and later to the writings of Malcom X.   Robinson himself had taught Afro-American history classes in a neighborhood church, and Bill Darden was steeped in the writings of Stephen Douglas and other historians of the black experience.

But more to the point, they felt that they had an education about the *world*, the way that life is really lived, which is denied to the graduates of the best schools and colleges.   Robinson took frequent delight in a public rehearsal of WSO's task of "educating white liberals" from the universities, seminaries, and upper middle class churches who came to WSO for months of training.   Poor blacks he argued, have a "mother wit" which can take them a long way even in this world.   Thus the charge of being uneducated for the work of driving a truck and conducting basic business operations was portrayed as an unsubtle means of keeping the black man in his place.

The rhetoric of WSO speeches was supplemented by actions which gave evidence of abilities which no formal education could certify. WSO men were being asked to speak before groups in other parts of the city and suburbs. Their words were recorded and printed in the WSO *Torch*, a biweekly newspaper that was circulated throughout the community. The paper itself, though written and edited in the early years by white volunteers and staff, represented a penetration by WSO into the public sphere where words and actions are scrutinized. (After 1967 *The Torch* was written and managed entirely by local people.)

As the campaign against Centennial began to attract the attention of the public media and other institutions, the leaders seized upon every opportunity to state their case and to become established figures who dealt face-to-face with other prominent people. Their alliances among the consultants and trainees in WSO and the leaders of important economic institutions in the city spoke volumes about their success in overcoming the deprivations of an inferior education.

In short, the "victimized" image was accepted, but reversed through public acts. Yes, WSO members *had* suffered the classic career of poor children denied a fair opportunity to study, learn, and ascend to responsibility in the economy and the community. But it had not been a passive nor ultimately debilitating suffering. They could act and communicate in the public forums. Needless to say, this rhetorical reversal worked even more strongly against characterizing formal educational weaknesses as "bad character."

The standard which demanded a continuous and satisfactory record of previous employment was also countered in WSO. The problem here was pervasively represented in characteriological terms. An employee deserving of reward and greater trust must have *proved himself* responsible and disciplined in the ways of work. But what meaning did those words convey? The word "responsible" in the middle class idiom meant an ability to manage funds, relationships, and tasks which the man who was poor and black had never been given. The jobs available to them were menial, boring, and dead end. As for "discipline," in 1964 there were simply too few examples within the system wherein just rewards came to the ordinary black man who worked most of his life with diligence and who practiced the classic virtue of deferred gratification. Robinson's rhetoric of "urban plantations," on which black people continued to labor for less than subsistence was apt. Meanwhile, the organization again provided evidence of what black leadership could do when provided with some funds and influence to manage. Responsibility and discipline might appear in a new guise that could make its own claims upon employers. WSO's assertion that it was able to qualify applicants for work in responsible positions did not seem audacious to those who thought they understood better than a white manager, or a bureaucrat, what qualities of manhood emerge from life in the black community.

The problem of criminality and the requirement for a "clean" record were also addressed, largely in the context of public meetings at WSO headquarters. The fact that WSO men had criminal records, including felony convictions, was interpreted to mean that they had paid for what they had done wrong, whereas a great many persons in the white community commit crimes for which they are never punished. In speeches and informal communications, WSO men seldom attempted excuses for what they had done and been punished for, although they

saw plenty of evidence that the courts had looked upon them with
racist eyes. This is an important point, and reflects again a
situation before the time when black criminality became widely interpreted as a function of racist oppression. The men of WSO did
not understand themselves as having been political prisoners. They
had broken laws and paid a price, sometimes an unfair price in
comparison with patterns of conviction among white criminals, but
now they were free of culpability, though not of the stigma which
unjustly continued. Being barred from significant employment because of a criminal record was obviously a perpetuation of that
injustice.

More positively, they used their new associations with the
clergy, businessmen, and others from "respectable" society as evidence that they were not pariahs, but worthy of confidence. They
took pains to interpret carefully their precise compliance with the
laws in whatever actions WSO undertook in furthering its cause.
Their representations were to be allowed no opportunity to offend
against the law and consciences of those who honored them.

WSO men seldom spoke about the marital problems of their fellows
and themselves, either in private to me or in public. When they did,
it was in terms of the difficulties a man faces in acting the role
of a good husband and father when it is so hard to get and keep a
good job. The employment standard at Centennial, that a man be
living in the bonds of marriage, was clearly a tough one to get
around. Ostensibly the standard was set to guarantee the stability
of the salesman, his likelihood of staying with the job, of keeping
out of trouble,and avoiding money problems at home which might pro-
voke irregularities in the way he handled company collections. This
kind of requirement probably functions in many firms and industries
where race is not an issue in hiring. Wherever it is enforced it
acts harshly upon men from the ranks of the poor for whom personal
and economic troubles seem ineluctably fused. Curiously, it is
not a widely enforced standard for persons in the higher reaches
of management and the professions, but this last observation played
no part in WSO's responses to the exclusion of the single males
from productive employment. The issue was, in fact, largely ignored.

Evidence of Responsibility

The public challenge launched by WSO against a prominent service
industry in the West Side community provoked a series of encounters
and engagements with other groups and institutions in the urban
society, each of which represented a different problem for the young
organization in establishing its own representative style. Because
WSO began as a project of the Urban Training Center in Chicago, an
organization with its own alliances in Protestant and other religious organizations in the city, and because the two white consultants, Keating and Strom, had been seconded to that project
while employed by the Chicago City Missionary Society, WSO was required to interpret its actions to a board of "community guardians"
who occupied high positions in the financial and industrial leadership of the city. Their perceptions of the "social problem" which
WSO represented differed enough from the standard ideology that they
were prepared to offer tentative support to this new experiment in
leadership development. Centennial Laundry was attacked as a target

symbolic of exploitation. But appeal to the white "guardians" was
a rhetorical strategy of ingratiation.

The problem presented was a difficult one. The nascent organization needed to maintain its representative identity among the very
poor of the community. There is evidence that the leaders of WSO
were wary of the commitments of the several white men who were
participating in the action, and suspicious of the strings that
were attached to all of them through the people and funds that came
from outside the ghetto. Yet it was the cadremen who found themselves reassuring others whom they brought into WSO from the streets
that the white ministers in WSO were on the level, and that there
was a real commitment to self-direction by the local people. The
strings that *were* attached did *not* control.

At the same time their claims upon the interest of the "downtown" whites could not be dissipated. The leaders needed to show
independence and militancy before their constituency on the Near
West Side, and yet exact a measure of respect from their restive
allies in the skyscrapers downtown. It is instructive to note at
the outset the kind of action they did *not* take.

Throughout the many long months of negotiations with the
"guardians," during which WSO was continuously engaged in interpreting and dampening rumors, alleviating suspicions, responding
to near threats of being cut adrift, etc., the leaders never moved
to the stage of confrontation, or showdown, with their allies. The
explanation for this can appear absurdly simple; they were afraid
to bite the hand that fed them. Yet matters were never quite that
elementary. (For many of the hardest months there was no financial
support coming to any one of the indigenous leaders, even though
the white consultants continued to draw their professional salaries.)
In the early years WSO was nearly always under hard pressure from
militant elements in the movement to purge themselves of their
associations with whites. Confrontation was in the air. But the
troublesome relationships with the white liberals on the CCMS Board
were a valued asset not to be squandered. WSO must be credited
with the sagacity to appreciate the several dimensions of self-
interest at stake, and with delaying indefinitely the gratifications
to be savored in blasting free of white entanglement.

In the meantime, as recounted in the story of the face-off with
ACT militants, WSO leaders, on their own merits, won a measure of
respect and some new commitments from their white allies. WSO also
gained some counters to use in their negotiations downtown. The
liberal establishment was committed to hearing WSO leaders because
of who they were and whom they represented. Other groups, like
the Alinsky-ite Woodlawn Organization (TWO), could adopt confrontation tactics, using the institutional power of a community in
some control of its latent political force. Other ghetto groups
which had begun to spring up in communities like the Near West Side,
but who had none of the ties with establishment forces that both
bind and nourish, could indulge in harsh ideological warfare. Their
counter was the vague implication that raw political power *might* be
latent within the much larger constituency of unorganized people
who could be led into action behind harsh militant leadership.
Meanwhile, WSO labored to preserve both their alliances *and* the
signs of viable independence.

The substance which bonded their precarious alliance was the
moral commitment of enlightened liberal churchmen to the sense of

right which the black leaders articulated. This kind of symbolic
power is, of course, very unstable, perhaps even ephemeral. It can
be expended easily, or uselessly dissipated. Or it can be nurtured
toward a constancy of real interdependence in interests and destinies.
WSO enacted a concern both to communicate a perspective for which
they felt responsible, and to avoid an accommodation of that perspective to their powerful white audiences. They had to experience
the fine line of difference between "checking with downtown" before
taking actions which they knew would be hard to accept in the liberal establishment, and maintaining essential lines of communication
--of eliciting sincere concern without control.

      After 1966, Black Power ideology entailed a form of confron-
tation of perspectives in which the white power group was required
to feel the intensity of alienation and disjunction between the
white world and the black. WSO was certainly an early militant
group in the Chicago scene. Its tactics of symbolic confrontation
with employers, the picketing of their plant,and the threat of a
buyers' boycott, were not easily received as strategies that har-
monize with liberal reforms. But WSO militancy was very pragmatic.
The requirement to "tell it like it is" entailed some responsibility
to enable certain audiences to "hear it like it is." Alienation of
whites for its own sake was not considered desirable or a necessary
strategy to establish WSO's credentials of militant leadership,
even though ACT and other exponents of a harsher rhetoric were on
the scene.

      WSO spokesmen, and Robinson in particular, accomplished their
strategy by keeping WSO concerns and demands very close to the
elemental needs of the people of the community. They resisted being
bound up in any "philosophies" such as they heard emanating from the
"preachers" and others who were seeking to build a national movement on various ideological grounds. They appealed instead to the
imaginative understanding of what was happening to the young men
who were going jobless in their middle thirties, to the youth who
were harassed by the police and driven from the streets in their
own neighborhoods, and to the welfare mothers who had no one to
protect them when their meagre support was suspended or threatened.
When they spoke compellingly of these things to rooms filled with
their own people and numerous visitors, or before suburban audiences
in church buildings, their "right" to act as advocates of the poor,
even in militant actions that went against the grain of "due process"
and "fair bargaining," was hard to deny. And when, suddenly, as in
the summer of 1966, in the middle of civil disorder, the police,
government, press, television, churches, citizenry, youth gangs,
and the civil rights leadership of the country, all descended upon
their particular neighborhood, looking for leadership and for net-
works of communal relationship, for sources of information and
opinion, then WSO's particular legitimacy as a representative authority became visible. In these ways WSO was regarded for a time
as the real bridge between communities which had seldom, if ever,
communicated with one another before.

The Meaning of the Means

      In nearly every action of WSO the alliance of "black and white
together" was portrayed. It was the policy from the outset that

black men were to lead WSO, choose their own goals, speak for themselves, but have at their side in every instance a white man who
represented the power black men were denied. This may seem a naive
and primitive act of manipulating symbols, but it introduced into
every meeting between WSO and other persons in authority, both
white and black, the issue of whether to speak to the white man
first, or to the black. When, as usual, the white WSO member was
addressed as the proper person to reckon with, the opportunity was
taken to insist that it was the black man to whom matters of importance must be directed. The black man was urged, against long
ingrained habit, to speak for himself, rather than stand back and
allow the white man to lead.

It meant also that in every public encounter the cadremen had
to deal with the issue of whether they were, or were not, "under
the thumb" of the white man. This question was sometimes put to
them outright by persons curious about the new organization and its
program, or by others who assumed that the presence of whites at
all levels meant the organization was tainted. The question was
agonized over in staff sessions as the increasingly subtle possibilities of control from beyond the community had to be confronted.
Probably it was a question the black leaders asked themselves
silently, but the method employed on each occasion where leadership
was tested required that the *issue* be engaged in an action setting,
rather than on ideological terms alone. Can blacks lead whites and
not be "taken in?"

Another means shaping the action of WSO was the community
meeting, the grievance sessions which WSO held every Wednesday
night during the Centennial dispute in their storefront headquarters
just a few doors away from the laundry's main plant. The grievance
session is often used in organizing a union or political group.
These gatherings, however, were not made up of workers within the
industry, but of community members, some of whom may have formerly
worked at Centennial, or who had relatives there, but most of whom
had no jobs at all. Very few of them were regular customers of the
laundry, for obvious economic reasons. In these meetings WSO was
gathering a constituency of the left-out. The effect was to shift,
to some extent, the meaning of who these people were and what they
represented. They were persons who bore the stigma of having no
worth because the economic power in their community declared them
to have none. The grievance sessions served to demonstrate that
the economic institution, Centennial Laundry, was itself discred-
ited. If its procedures were revealed as illegal, dishonest, or
wicked, then its power to grant or deny status was also denigrated.

This rather obvious analysis need not ignore the bread and
butter issues actually at stake in the Centennial issue. But the
fact was that few, if any, of those who came to WSO grievance
meetings, or participated in the picketing and protests, would ever
reap economic advantages from a change in that institution's
policies. Welfare mothers might hope that their sons might some-
day earn eight to ten thousand dollars per year driving a truck for
Centennial, but for most of them the meetings were an exercise in
the reinterpretation of the symbols of power and worth as they
operated in that community.

The community gatherings served another purpose in those early
months of activity, one which had disappeared by the time my own
observations began in 1965. Plans and strategy were discussed and

ratified in the open meeting. Demands were decided upon and the
next moves were plotted. Even then, to be sure, a great amount of
strategic planning took place in the staff sessions,and gradually
the decision-making function of the open meeting became a ceremonial
acceptance of staff decisions. But even as this tendency toward
narrower control increased, the public decision-making process remained the counter with which WSO cadremen played for more time,
avoiding hard commitments in bargaining and mediating sessions with
outside agents. The staff could not act, it could argue for the
"community," and all decisions had to be returned to the Wednesday
night gathering for discussion and decision.

This process disturbed the white consultants and other volunteers from outside the community itself for whom a strong principle
was at stake. The founding vision of WSO was one in which the power
to lead was reposed in "the people," meaning the poor and disinherited. Keating and others frequently expressed distress and dis-
appointment over the gradual disappearance of real decision-making
from the community as a whole. This conflict of ideology within
the WSO inner circle was clearly evident in the confusion over the
actual election of a white seminarian to serve as the first chairman of the community council. In this instance the white consultants intervened to realign WSO polity with the populist ideology
of the outsiders, thus deflecting for a time the strategy of leadership desired by the cadremen. But before very long even the elected
members of the community council were obliged to style their participation after that of the leaders in order to participate in the
decision-making--that is, they were required to join in the actions
and be present when the staff debated the issues, rather than to
sit in a formal assembly of representatives elected to govern.

For the cadremen, who eventually ceased bothering with the
process of referring decisions to the community meeting, the for-
mality of laying their plans before the community retained significance. It was a means of exemplifying their leadership skills and
testing responses.

These developments which redefined the character of order and
representativeness within WSO meant different things to various
observers and critics of the WSO experiment. Very early in the process Saul Alinsky warned Archie Hargraves against this style of
organizing which concentrated upon the under class of a lower class
community. It would, he said, split the larger community instead
of bringing it together. It would seem undeniable that his prophecy
was correct. For those early advocates of WSO who looked to it as
a means of enlisting the numerical strength of the dispossessed,
drawing inspiration and leadership from their ranks, and consoli-
dating the masses behind authentic representatives of the people,
WSO was a source of disillusionment, almost from the outset. What
was not comprehended by those who affirmed the original vision is
that the process of forming a polity on the ground of identities
which are discovered as they emerge from action defines the markers
of exclusion as well as inclusion.

WSO was a probe directed at finding and enabling leaders with
styles and perspectives indigenous to the streets, who would act
within the world on matters that affected them most deeply. The
result was that these leaders rejected organizational forms which
threatened their style of personal influence among those with whom
they were "tight." Authentic representative leaders were found,

but their leadership could be exercised only within ∪ circle defined
by *their* trust and feeling of oneness.

New Roles — Advocates

The documentary material on the development of the welfare
union supports several observations:
The work of welfare organizing provided plenty of action and
a minimum of routine. The real action involved making a direct
representation of the case in the welfare office. At first these
deputations were undertaken in strength, with several of the
brothers, plus one or two white preachers (who had both cars and
collars--extremely helpful for moving through street and bureaucratic traffic). The case described at length earlier, wherein more
than a dozen people carried out the assignment for two women at the
Englewood District Office, was certainly a *tour de force*, an exag-
geration for effect, but a clear example of what strength was behind even a minor effort. After the routine of representation became established, the ordinary complaint from a recipient was taken
care of with one or two WSO agents accompanying the women to the
welfare office. For many cases the procedure was eventually reduced
to a telephone call to a trusted supervisor and perhaps to the case
worker.
The point is that this direct representation was an action the
brothers of WSO undertook together. It depended upon the solidarity
they had established with one another and upon the expertise they
shared in knowing how to handle each case. It was a different kind
of work than they had known before. The work force in which they
had previous experience required that they separate themselves from
the people--the sights and sounds of their milieu--and become individuals in another kind of orientation--one governed by a time clock,
and by standards of operation and efficiency enforced most often by
white foremen or supervisors. To work with WSO was to remain a
ghetto man, to work alongside the brothers, to employ the strength
of that association in solving some of the "bread and butter" problems of their sisters in the ghetto.
The welfare union action provided intimations of a different
kind of relationship between ghetto men and women, one which depended
upon the men having some access to the power that could affect ma-
terially the lives of the women and children. WSO's welfare organizers
were able to display a self-acquired knowledge of the complicated
workings of the welfare system which few, if any, of the recipients
had ever attained. They knew something about the informal and formal procedures in the various district offices; they knew persons
here and there who were predictably sympathetic or antagonistic to
the type of case presented; and they had mastered the provisions
in the welfare code which provided an opening for the recipient to
make claims of inadequate support or shabby treatment, instead of
being completely the suppliant of the welfare professionals. This,
plus the readiness of the cadre to act together to force welfare
into a position of compliance with their demands, meant that the
men of WSO assumed a new importance and authority in the community,
especially with the women whom they helped directly. Whether or
not one considers these matters in the context of the alleged problems of emasculation suffered by many black males in our society,

one very obvious factor of the ghetto mother's predicament is her
economic vulnerability, and one grave difficulty for the ghetto
male who may wish to be respected as the head of a family is his
inability to be economically productive. WSO provided a way for
black men to function as advocates and providers for dependent
women, and to achieve a measure of esteem in their eyes for dcing
so.

To process a welfare complaint required first that the complainant, almost always a woman with children, provide answers to a
series of approximately a dozen questions, which were noted by the
interviewer on a form. This form was used as a record of the complaint and its resolution but was also the means for the union
activists to pursue the needs of the woman in the welfare office
responsible for her case. The form asked for the name, address,
and family circumstances of the woman, including the name of each
child and the means of support, other than welfare, that might be
forthcoming for the child. The form sought the greatest detail in
asking the woman to report her experiences with the Department of
Public Welfare--the name of the case worker and supervisor, the
budget details which were the basis of her money grant from the
Department, and the nature of her complaint.

Without requiring the interviewer to probe for the intimate
circumstances of her life, the WSO interview provided an absorbing
experience of hearing and sharing vital human concerns in an atmosphere of surprising openness and trust. As a white man calling
on welfare complainants with John Crawford, or taking the information myself in the welfare union office, or in the complainant's
home, I found only one person among the eighty or so I interviewed
who expressed a reluctance to answer the questions. Meanwhile,
the men of WSO gave sustained and careful attention to this interview procedure, although they had no training in this kind of
activity except as interviewees in schools, jails, agencies, and
welfare. They proved themselves to be able and sympathetic listeners, patient in enabling a woman to express herself, and helpful
in clarifying the often complicated circumstances in which she felt
wronged and in need of help from the union.

The woman usually found in the interviewer a person who was
sympathetic and who was not trying to spot some irregularity or
some attempt to bilk the public treasury. Moreover, the man encouraged her to believe that something could be done, through her
effort and his, to break through an intolerable and seemingly hope-
less situation. By their own reports, these persons sensed in the
WSO worker one who knew from his own experience something of the
desperateness of their lives. They expressed the feeling that it
was an entirely different experience for them to go for assistance
to someone who was poor and black like themselves, and to receive
assurance that something *would* be done.

Thus we can observe in the welfare union activities the creation
of behavior which was often deeply satisfying for both the men and
the women. For the men the gratifications were those of being en-
trusted with confidences and with the means to provide genuine
assistance, for which genuine gratitude was returned. For the
women the experience was one of being treated by a man with sympathy and respect and of having some of their pressing needs fulfilled. One can speak meaningfully of a new kind of dignity experienced in this context. In dramatistic terms the character

iological dimensions of motivations are featured most clearly.

The account of the development of WSO's welfare union indicates that WSO was able to put its finger upon two aspects of the recipients' psychological predicament which had immobilized and restrained them from participation in activities which might have helped them deal with their personal and political problems. I refer to the twin enemies of fear and ignorance. Their fear was of the alleged power of the case worker, the supervisor, and even the precinct captain--powers to withhold the all-important welfare check in exchange for correct behavior on the part of the recipients. The ignorance was of the actual provisions of the complicated welfare code wherein they were protected from exactly those threats of which they were most fearful, and in which their actual rights--including, in some cases, the right to a higher level of support--were prescribed.

Our interviews showed that these fears had their basis in reality. Time after time the complaint was heard, "My check has been cut off [or withheld], and I have no way to feed my children." A call to the welfare office was usually enough to verify the complaint and to insist that the money be provided *at once*, appealing, if necessary, to the Code's simple provision wherein the Department of Public Aid is charged with *guaranteeing* that no child should suffer from want. Sometimes the crisis was created by a case worker withholding a check in an effort to enforce compliance with one or another directive from the Department. ·More often the delay was due to the incredibly complicated bureaucratic snarls and missteps that occur in the system, for which the client and her children endured untold suffering.

A case worker might use a discretionary power (sometimes assumed and implemented unilaterally by simply refusing to process promptly a recipient's applications) in one of the following typical ways:

    a.   The woman allegedly had other possible means of support which, in the case worker's judgment, she was refusing to identify or to exert herself to obtain. This could mean that the woman, again in the case worker's view, had not done as much as she could do to force the father of her child(ren) to pay support regularly. What actual recourse the woman might have to force support from the man varied immensely and could hardly be realistically adjudged by a case worker only marginally acquainted with the persons and the facts of the case.

    b.   The recipient had misspent her budgetary allowance, as when money designated for rent or for gas had been used for other purposes. Not infrequently this "poor budgeting" was the result of an emergency in the family for which funds were needed immediately. Nevertheless, until the summer of 1966, the case worker could require such designated monies be paid directly in disbursement checks to the landlord, the gas company, etc., a process which often required bureaucratic adjustments resulting in delays of several days of the precious welfare check.

    c.   The woman had refused to take work, or to undergo training for work, which the case worker assumed she was able to do. It was, after all, the case worker's directive to get the family off the public support and onto self-support as soon

as possible. It was by no means uncommon to find cases
where an able-bodied woman with small children was being
required to take work, or "rehabilitation" training, regardless of whether or not she preferred to be at home with
her children.

d. A woman, having left the welfare rolls for a time because
she had taken a job, or was living with a man who could
give her support, was having difficulty "getting back on
aid," for reasons which it was the prerogative of the case
worker to evaluate. If a job had been lost, explanations
and justifications were in order. If the woman had been
deserted, wasn't it possible for her to get the man back,
whether or not she wanted him around? In the meantime,
all important requisitions for aid were delayed for weeks
at a time.

e. The recipient was being transferred from one category of
welfare to another, a procedure which might mean being
assigned a new case worker, a new budget, and even a new
district office from which she would receive her funds.
Again, it was not uncommon for this to occur without the
recipient understanding why the change was being made, or
even that it *was* being made.

In the category of sheer bureaucratic foul-ups, the following are
typical instances of delayed payment:

a. A case worker abruptly resigns from the Department and his
case load is not yet reassigned. (Actually the yearly
turnover in the Department was staggering, and there was
always a shortage of case workers.) If the case worker
left with some matter requiring approval hanging in the
air, the recipient could count on *no* action until a new
case worker was on the scene and in touch with her particular case.

b. Inter-office delays between the Cook County Department and
the State Office were routine, especially where changes in
status for the recipient required the shifting of budgetary
categories, and even funding sources, as when an ADC mother,
whose funds were under a national welfare provision, was
shifted to General Assistance, which was somehow more
locally administered.

c. Sheer confusion in the overtaxed welfare offices.

Thus the fears of the recipient were grounded in having to con-
front alone the inefficiencies and immobility of a huge bureaucracy
and in alienating the case worker or petty officials, who were able
to put her "out of touch with that money." In the first type of
situation WSO's strong representation in the welfare office was inevitably successful in forcing the sluggish machinery to move at a
very accelerated rate indeed. Checks were demanded of case work
supervisors and district supervisors, under the emergency provisions
of the Code, if necessary, and the welfare union organizer usually

stayed with the client until a check or disbursing order was in her
hands.

In the second type of circumstance, the client's fear of her
case worker was alleviated by WSO's demonstration that it could go
over the head of the case worker in nearly any district office and
demand attention to the case. Some case workers were very irked
about WSO's interference in their relationship with the client, but
in no case reported was there an effective retaliation on the part
of the case worker against a client for her action in resorting to
WSO representation. In a few instances, WSO interceded for the
client in having her case transferred to another case worker entirely.

Some clients told WSO that their case worker had warned them
against joining the welfare union and had told them that WSO was
not recognized by the Department. This was true, of course, in so
far as official policy was concerned. When William Robinson became
Director of Public Aid, WSO received strong personal endorsement
and signs of approval from the head office, but the official recognition of WSO's right to sit as a third party in the grievance
hearing was established early in the game, and was all the legitimation WSO required to "represent" its client members. A number
of case workers did not resent WSO's effort on behalf of their
clients and were glad to receive the added assistance in pushing
the agency for better service.

Perhaps WSO's most important innovation for welfare recipients
was convincing them, in many cases at least, that the welfare Code
was their charter of rights, which they could learn to use in their
own situations and in those of friends. Case work policy which
assumes the goal and the desirability of removing people from welfare rolls must be secondary to the principle that the recipient's
essential needs, and those of dependents, must be met. The threat
of removing the recipient from aid in order to obtain compliance
is ultimately and legally unenforceable, regardless of how case
workers evaluate the recipient's record.

As a matter of tactic, WSO taught the recipients that they
should expect their case workers to use every means possible to get
them off of aid because of the constant pressure upon the Department from taxpayers, lawmakers, etc., to cut the relief rolls. But
the personal interests of the recipient were primary, legally and
morally, and the recipient had the right to insist on the full
letter of the Code's support. To be sure, the union affirmed that
no one would want to be on aid if there were a reasonable alternative to it, but a reasonable alternative did not mean forcing a
woman to take work, if that required that she leave her children
every day. The threat of some case workers that a woman would lose
her aid if she refused to go for employment training, or to take
work found for her by the Department, could be an empty threat.
WSO backed up scores of women in their refusals to be taken out of
their homes in order to relieve the burden of welfare on society.

The fear of retribution from a precinct captain, or some other
petty political figure, was one problem which WSO could not con-
front directly, except to assure the client that ultimately the
threat could not be carried out, as long as the welfare union was
available to pursue the matter. Moreover, when William Robinson
became Director he made frequent public pledges, including television statements, that the welfare rights of any recipient so

intimidated would be protected.

In the intake interview, the one area of importance to the poor person seeking aid wherein WSO had no legal avenue to provide representation, the influence of WSO in some of the district offices was of direct help in "interpreting" the case and speeding up the application procedures. The organizers were sometimes helpful, also, in assisting persons having trouble meeting the long list of requirements for receiving sustenance from the State of Illinois by transporting them to various offices for birth certificates, court affidavits, etc.

All of this educative activity must be seen as an effort to create a new polity of informed citizens: to enable persons to act in the public world in the area most directly affecting their lives and well being. The fact that heretofore the system of public welfare was not considered to be an area in which recipients were expected to assert their rights and needs as citizens, because they were regarded as wards of the state, only proves the correctness of the claim that welfare has functioned to keep people subservient and dependent. Their only choice was to comply or refuse to comply and suffer the loss of their support.

But welfare has become a way of life for hundreds of thousands. Its policies and its administration are the immediate political realities with which the recipient families contend, just as industrial management was the chief political and economic reality for the industrial workers of America in the earlier decades of this century. WSO began a process of politicization, of political enfranchisement of persons who had been without any role as citizens, because they had not qualified within our system as productive wage earners. The welfare union concept was an attempt to widen the political representation of the poor by equipping them to deal with the realities of their difficult social situation. It may be evaluated, therefore, as a promising innovation in social organization in our time.

The welfare union introduced a pattern of mutuality among the women, based upon their common dilemma, plus the opportunity to receive immediate assistance with some of their problems. The assistance was, in large part, ameliorative rather than curative. But it pointed to a type of communal structure which might flow from vigorous, imaginative, and (most important, considering WSO limitations) well-supported efforts at organizing recipients and giving them responsibilities to act on behalf of one another.

In all of this it must be said that the welfare union was a noble experiment that did not finally fulfill its initial promise. The few WSO men handling the rush of complaints found themselves unable to sustain the day-to-day action, which eventually became routine. WSO could have used a hundred people processing complaints, but it needed another entire core of persons to do organization follow-up among the recipient members. Instead, five or six men, plus a few volunteers from outside the community, were all that were working at one time. Scores of cases were taken and their complaints resolved every month for more than one year. But unless the woman was exceptionally motivated by what she had experienced in WSO, she was allowed to disappear into her private life and was seldom seen again. The few women who caught hold and devoted themselves to the organization proved their potential. But not enough was done to sustain the drive. No organizational structure capable

of utilizing the full vision glimpsed in the early months of welfare
unionism came into being.

New Roles — Spokesmen and Interpreters

The actions of the WSO leadership during the crisis in the Near
West Side community should be interpreted as responses for which
no previous preparation or intentional strategy had been developed.
The leadership of WSO had never planned or discussed how it ought to
respond to civil disorder occurring in its own community. Yet
opportunities to lead, to act as protectors and mediators, as interpreters and spokesmen, emerged during a few troubled hours of
crisis.   This section of the analysis deals with those motivations
which arose from the means which WSO possessed to act within a situation wherein neither their own conscious strategies, their particular characteriological qualifications, nor the conditions of
their background determined the dimensions of action.

WSO claimed that in a civil crisis its representative style
gave its leaders access to and influence among some of the West
Side citizens that no other leadership, official or otherwise, could
provide.   The fact is that the leaders of WSO became involved in the
conflict initially because the police asked their assistance in controlling a situation in which larger disorder was threatened.   Every
public act thereafter was directed toward ending or preventing the
spread of violence.   What is noteworthy for our interests are the
resources used by the leaders in pursuing this course.

First in importance was their visibility as indigenous young
men of the community, in whom some trust had been vested.   They were
able to take responsibility for action in a crisis.   The stance of
WSO among the people of the neighborhood as a group militantly
favoring the poor in their struggles was, by this time, understood,
however much it may have been resented or suspected by some.

Important to this stance was the fact that the leaders were
not perceived as proponents of an ideology that required adoption
of a correct or superior moral strategy if the people were to be
assisted in their struggles.   WSO's *message* was that the *organization* reflected the needs of the people directly and immediately.
WSO was not selling an interpretation of their victimization which
required reinterpretation into abstract political or idealistic
forms.   Thus when Robinson, Darden, or Crawford spoke to the people
during those days of crisis,they recognized the people's grievances
but also drew attention to the inconsequential and self-destructive
nature of the riot.   They did not hesitate to identify the cause
of the people's anger as the intolerant, inept, and even cruel behavior of the police.   But this did not impel them to advocate a
strategy of nonviolence in conflict with the police, nor to turn
to the self-defense tactics espoused by the militants.   The tactic
was to cool the riot because of the harm the people were suffering,
to enable the people to articulate their grievances within the situation, and counteract the versions of the riot which had appeared
in the press and on television.

WSO men performed their roles by doing several things they do
very well: they spoke in public passionately and directly; they
walked and talked with the people; they sang and fought; they kept
their counsel with friends and confidants, and they dealt openly

with strangers and adversaries. They acknowledged the help of outside leaders who had stature within the community--King, Young,
and others--but they did not forfeit their own hold upon the leadership of the community, including the ability to interpret correctly
its mood and responses.

Thus the larger public role of protectors and guardians of the
peace was assumed by young men who, before the formation of WSO,
would have been among the last to be called upon by the police, and
who would not have been in any position to employ the means they
used to quell the trouble. Their roles as mediators and interpreters
were acknowledged by nearly every group or agency that became involved in the crisis and its resolution--the gangs, the ministers,
the media, the church leaders of the city, the civil rights forces,
and the citizens of the Near West Side community. Only the political structure seemed disinclined to consult, depend on, or draw
attention to the young community organization on the Near West
Side, although a few years later the negative evaluation of the
influence of police power within the black community was acknowledged by established political leaders of that community in Chicago.

A Higher Authority

Finally, there are several elements of WSO's rhetorical strategy
that emerge from its rather problematic relationship with the leadership of the Chicago freedom movement in the summer of 1966. Unless
they are clearly identified, it is difficult to resist an interpretation of these events which suggests that the men of WSO were
simply overwhelmed by the presence of local figures whose prominence
was city wide. It may well be that jealousies and fears were indeed
influential in these matters, but other symbolic motives were func-
tioning as well, and to these our interest is directed.

It will be convenient to locate these rhetorical themes by referring to selected parts of Robinson's long and extemporaneous
address a portion of which is reproduced in the previous chapter,
bearing in mind that it was delivered to a packed gathering of in-
tensely interested people at WSO in the week following WSO's repudi-
ation of the summit agreement. Except for the first days of the riot
on the Near West Side in the month preceding, this was the time of
highest tension and excitement within WSO.

Robinson began: "I don't know what to say." After this he
spoke for a full hour! He acknowledged the very worst that had
been said about himself and the WSO leadership in the public press
and also within the counsels of the movement.

> Folks been talking about us like we was dogs. You don't pay no
> attention to that. They talked about Jesus Christ.

Many of the "folks" who had been talking about WSO's perfidy were
ministers who were active in the Chicago freedom movement. It must
be remembered that WSO was constantly in trouble with ministers of
the Near West Side, black and white. And now other bearers of this
religious authority were joining in. But the people must remember,
said Robinson, that these same types of people attacked Jesus Christ.

He said, "Father forgive them. They don't know what they're doing."
I ain't going to say that.

The audacious identification of WSO with the sacred personage was
made and then suddenly reversed. It would not do to claim too much
of the martyr's role, as if WSO people were saintly figures. They
were common poor people, without even the graces of the middle class,
much less the power to forgive.
Robinson next told the moving story of the man who could not
obtain his rightful salary check after having left the hospital.
Again the religious theme was daringly ventured. The man got on
his knees and asked for God's direction, and was led to WSO. Did
he find saints ready to help? No, he found Robinson, who was too
busy to pay attention and thought the man was probably drunk. But
others took him in hand, and the man's need was filled.
This is what counts! This is the whole thing that counts! It
is the help received in WSO in desperate circumstances. It comes
when brothers act together in response to need. One cannot go it
alone, any more than a man can move into a nearly rent-free house
in Cicero alone. One must move with one's own and act with strength.

Now they say when we get all of this [the summit agreement] they
going to open all of the city. Now, I don't see no *doors* on the
city anywhere. I don't know what they mean by opening up the city.
Let all them middle class people move where they want to move.

By contrast with what WSO does in meeting the immediate needs
of the people, the summit agreement offered something that poor
people couldn't even understand. They could not understand it because they knew something the negotiators did not know--that the
city cannot be opened up by an agreement, as if it were a matter
of opening a door. That will not change the hatred of the whites
for the poor blacks. Robinson's own mother knew that when she saw
the behavior of people in the white neighborhoods that Dr. King was
trying to open up with marches. Maybe the middle class black
people could make it out there. Then let them do it. The real
problem was in the places where the poor people lived even as he
spoke.

But you know, people will say anything to indoctrinate you. But I
don't believe in philosophies, and doctrination.... Jesus had that
fish and that bread.... And I believe we can do a whole lot with
our basic problems.

This was one of Robinson's favorite themes. It was not true
that he did not understand the ideas and philosophies of the movement, for he had been a keen student of Afro-American history and
the teachings of Garvey, DuBois, and Malcom X. But he knew that
it was possible for people to style themselves as leaders because
they had learned to articulate these "philosophies." This did not
count as real leadership, because "philosophies" enable one to
screen out the everyday "bread and butter" concerns of people.
Thus Robinson fostered a distrust of many of those movement
leaders who identified themselves with the cause of the people.
Again he was particularly hard on the black ministers. The wearing
of old clothes, by those who had no need to do so, unsuccessfully

masked a desire to act in exalted leadership roles which were jus-
tified on high moral and humanitarian grounds. Robinson declared
that his followers would dress up in their *good* clothes when they
went to represent the poor in the counsels of the mighty, since it
would be perfectly clear to Mayor Daley who the poor people really
were. It was the power of the poor that represented the real challenge, not the power of the high-minded and articulate "spokesmen
of the people."

> I'm not talking about Dr. King, 'cause Dr. King really does all the
> preaching and hard work.

Robinson would not dissociate WSO from the figure of King, but
from those around him, who didn't "represent" anybody. It was important that WSO be identified as part of that large drama being
played out in the streets, in the public media, and in the councils
of the city. The WSO man must be seen as one who could deal with
Dr. King and his lieutenants, with the national press and television,
and with representatives of corporate power in the city. WSO would
not cut itself off from the movement in Chicago, symbolized by Dr.
King, but would maintain its identity and freedom of action within
it. The target of Cicero was claimed by WSO for its own bargaining
purposes, not with the counselors at the summit, but with Dr. King,
who very much needed discipline in the ranks of the freedom forces.

> What I call a sell-out is when you get to a table, and you sit down
> with somebody and you say, "*My* people needs this. *My* people needs
> that." I don't think anybody here seen a thing in those agreements
> that will benefit you. So evidently somebody down there didn't
> know what their people needed. So they hadn't any business down
> there negotiating saying, "My people nothing."

> Big people fight over little people. That is how wars start. They
> don't start over money. Who is going to control these folks, and
> who is going to control the other folks? And they fight to see who
> is going to control, who has the power. And here *you* got all the
> power. So we are going to control *ourselves*.

Robinson then asked for a "consensus" on his proposals to be presented to Dr. King in exchange for the promise not to march into
Cicero. He didn't allow for a dissenting vote, "....cause I don't
want to hate nobody!"
     Certainly the actions of WSO and the words of its most prom-
inent leader illustrate the ambiguities of appeals to higher goals
and ultimate authority that were present in this charged situation.
The larger "movement" which had been activated in Chicago by the
presence of Martin Luther King Jr. and his most prominent lieutenants
legitimated their actions in regard to open housing on grounds of
deepest human right and highest religious authority. WSO's highly
publicized defection from the movement ranks, at the moment when a
"victory" in Chicago was being signaled by Dr. King himself, meant
that Robinson had to establish his position in terms which claimed
that authority in a truer interpretation of its meaning for the
people.
     It is hardly necessary to point out that Robinson did *not* (as
many militant defectors were doing) pronounce upon the irrelevancy

of the religious themes that were at the heart of the movement's ideology. In the summer of 1966 "Black Power" was being widely interpreted as a threat to the nonviolent crusaders of the civil rights forces in Chicago and elsewhere. Robinson, however, tried to forge a position within the ethos of religious feeling and conviction, but yet distant from that of his enemies and detractors among King's followers, the preachers and others whom he regarded as fellow travelers and traffickers in the dynamics of the disinherited.

Conclusion

As I noted in the Preface to this work, the years since the events recorded here have brought vast changes--death to the great American leader whose life touched many people in this story (without whom, indeed, the story itself and the accomplishments it notes would never have occurred), national office and prominence to some of his most able followers, grave and debilitating illness to the most remarkable of the leaders in WSO, Chester Robinson, and now charges of criminal acts against some of the cadremen who stayed with WSO through phases of its existence which seem to have little to do with the matters I have examined. Perhaps most remarkable, and, from my point of view, discouraging (apart from the personal tragedies of individuals I had come to know) is the shift in general ethos within our society, so that it has become doubtful whether even a very modest effort, like that of WSO, to enable a group of obscure people to speak and act in their own behalf would gain our attention. The very welcome fact that societal changes have opened channels of employment, residential neighborhoods, and representative processes to many black Americans should not blind us to the reality that the war against obscurity for the constituency of WSO was never seriously fought. The dismal statistics on hard core poverty, unemployment, bodily illness, victimization by criminals, fear and dependency, are still the indices by which the lives of the very poor are interpreted--that is, whenever they are noticed at all. Only now, because of the positive social changes that are visible to us all, it is even easier to believe that the very poorest of America's black, white, and Latin citizens are that way because they are incapable, or because they are bad.

Twelve years after the founding of WSO as a test-case in self-determination for the unemployable rejects of the productive society, the test would seem to have proved negative. But this study suggests that certain other conclusions ought to be entertained. The test was not serious enough. WSO provided intimations of a resourcefulness that, with greater patience and attention to the processes of self-determination exemplified in the group, might have been fostered and devoted to more constructive ends. But because it was born in the context of a movement, WSO was too quickly judged by many who were caught up in the dynamics of reform as not in harmony with the larger and often unrealistic ends which the movement ideology proposed. By the same token, it was judged by others to be a threat to the orderly administration of programs for the poor communities that depend upon professional expertise and political support.

WSO acted most responsibly when it was involved in its own particular ideological mission, to speak *from* dimensions of experience which it could represent (at least in part) *to* other audiences in the city who were interested, for a brief time only, in understanding what they had to say.

The process of interpretation depends upon creating and sustaining the structures which engage both parties in the difficult tasks of speaking and hearing. When one side or the other becomes indifferent, when the process itself becomes too costly in time, money, and effort, the accountability ends. What remains is a group of actors for whom the stake they have won in the community must be defended. Actions become more opportunistically circumscribed and finally defeating. The public sphere in which they were accorded the privilege of attention is depleted, though it hardly notices their absence. They remain present in the public consciousness, not as actors, but as elements in a scenic background characterized according to the symbols of deviance.

NOTES AND REFERENCES

1. Michael Clarke, "Social Problem Ideologies," *British Journal of Sociology*, 26 (1975): 406-16.

2. See the following representative discussions: Charles A. Valentine, *Culture and Poverty* (Chicago: University of Chicago Press, 1968); Edward C. Banfield, *The Unheavenly City* (Boston: Little, Brown, 1970); Oscar Lewis, "The Culture of Poverty," S.M. Miller and Marlin Rein, "Poverty and Social Change" and "Poverty and Self-Indulgence," in *Poverty in America*, ed. Louis A. Ferman (Ann Arbor: University of Michigan Press, 1951); Walter B. Miller, "Lower Class Culture as a Generating Milieu of Gary Delinquency," *Journal of Social Issues* 45, No. 3 (1958): 5-19; Elliot Lulow, *Talley's Courner* (Boston: Little, Brown, 1967).

3. Norman Bonvey, "Work and Ghetto Culture," *British Journal of Sociology*, 26 (1975): 435-47.

4. *Ibid.*, p. 444.

5. See H. Richard Niebuhr, *The Responsible Self* (New York: Harper & Row, 1963), p. 87.

6. Kenneth Burke, *A Grammar of Motives* (Berkeley and Los Angeles: University of California Press, 1969).

7. Hugh Dalziel Duncan, *Symbols in Society* (London: Oxford University Press, 1963).

8. William H. Rueckert, *Kenneth Burke* (Minneapolis: University of Minnesota Press, 1963).

9. Duncan, *Symbols in Society*, p. 61.

10. *Ibid.*, p. 64.

11. *Ibid.*, p. 70.

STUDIES IN RELIGION AND SOCIETY

edited by

Thomas C. Campbell, W. Alvin Pitcher,
W. Widick Schroeder and Gibson Winter

Order from your bookstore or the Center for the Scientific Study of Religion

Order from your bookstore